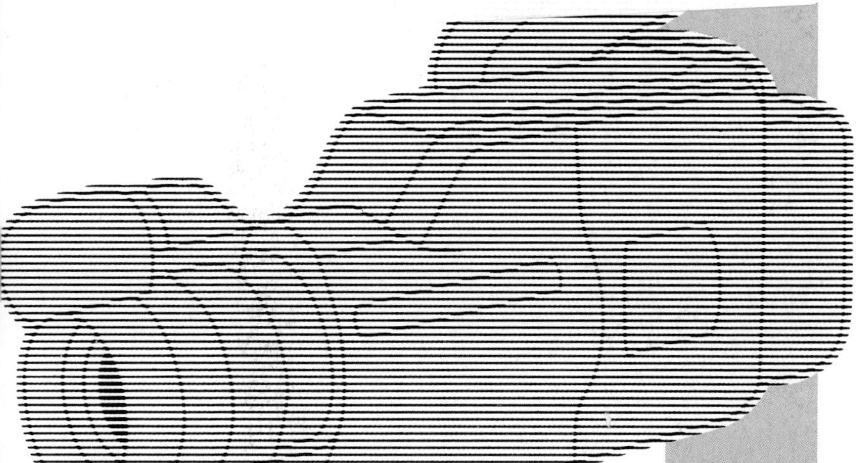

SONY CAMCORDERS

Harry Hennings

NIKON
RICOH
FUJI
YASHICA SAMURAI

HOVE FOTO BOOKS

Sony Camcorders

First English Edition August 1991
Published by Hove Foto Books
34 Church Road, Hove, Sussex BN3 2GJ

Englisch Translation: Petra Kopp
Technical Editor: Adrian Deary
Production Editor: Georgina Fuller
Typesetting & Layout: Annida's Written Page, Sussex BN15 0NR
Printed in Germany by Bosch Druck, Landshut

British Library Cataloguing in Publication Data
Hennings, Harry
Sony Camcorder
1. Video recorders
I. Title II. [Video Praxis Sony Camcorder]. *English*
621.38833

ISBN 0-906447-87-9

UK Distribution:

Newpro (UK) Ltd.
Old Sawmills Road
Faringdon, Oxon
SN7 7DS

Contents

Foreword

Video filming has become a popular hobby over recent years. A new era for amateur film-makers began with the introduction of handy camcorders, that is video cameras with an integrated recording unit. The simple, synchronized recording of image and sound with camcorders, which themselves were becoming smaller and smaller and easier to handle, together with the facility of instant play-back, added a new dimension to leisure-time filming. But despite the most modern technology, sophisticated automatic controls and simple handling, a few basic things need to be considered in videography in order to avoid possible problems. This handbook addresses those readers who already own a camcorder and are looking for information to help them make even more of their video films, as well as those who want to find out about the possibilities of video in general terms before buying a camcorder. Specialist authors have co-operated on this book and have contributed their experience and technical knowledge on the subject of video. It was the common goal of all the authors to demonstrate and explain the most important basic rules of video filming in a way that is practical and relevant. The analysis and description of heavy technical data has been deliberately avoided - those areas are covered by the operating manuals. Instead, this handbook sets out to explain clearly and comprehensively the meaning of technical features for video filming in practice. The first part is devoted to the different camcorders in the Sony family, giving an overview of their specific characteristics, particular features and abilities, and the effects these have in practical terms. The next section describes practical filming problems and their solutions, ranging from the correct way of holding the camcorder to production planning. It covers the drawing up of scripts or storyboards, the preparation and execution of recordings, giving tips for scene sequences, camera settings, lighting and direction.

"Despite sophisticated automatic controls, several basic things need to be considered in videography"

This advice for actual filming is followed by tips on the re-working of image and sound, that is, the order in which recorded scenes go into a video that makes it worth seeing. This section describes the simple electronic joining together of scenes, as well as sophisticated editing techniques with modern edit controllers and video processors.

One essential problem in video filming is that of sockets/jacks, plugs and adaptors. As so often in life, everything can depend on the right connections. What goes with what and how, and how you can make the best connections is also covered in detail. A further chapter is concerned with trouble-shooting. It describes the most frequent problems and gives tips on how they can be avoided and remedied. Camcorders have become popular with people who travel. But other countries don't just have different customs, they also have different television standards. This handbook will help guide you as to the correct usage of your camcorder when travelling. It ends with a comprehensive encyclopedia of the most used technical terms.

This handbook sets out to convey comprehensive basic technical knowledge on the subject of camcorders, but our hints and tips are also designed to help you achieve better video recordings, and to increase your enjoyment of this exciting new hobby.

We hope you have a lot of fun reading the handbook, and that it will become a valuable guide which can help you make as many impressive video films as possible. It has served its purpose even if it only tempts you to try one or two tips in practice. But however true or helpful the hints collected here may be, it is the same for videography as for photography in that practice makes perfect.

Harry Hennings

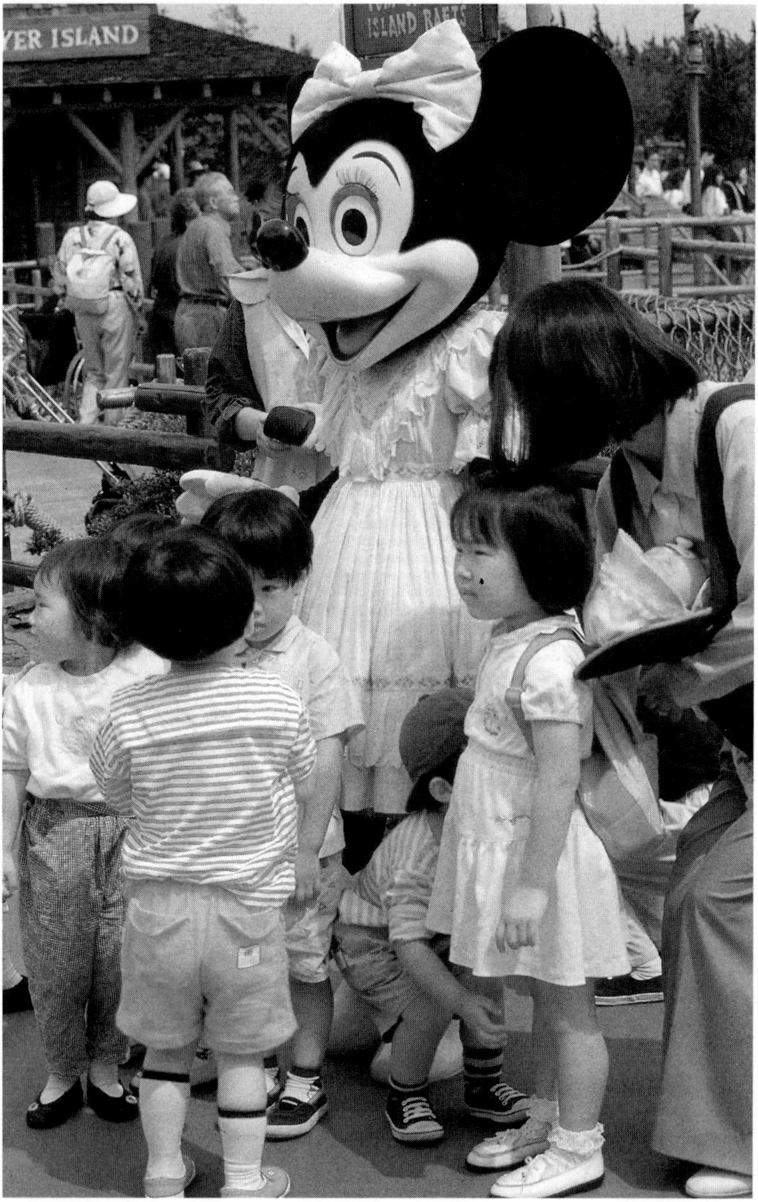
YER ISLAND
ISLAND RAFTS

The Sony Camcorder Family

'It's a Sony'- one of the best known advertising slogans which has seen such successful inventions as the Walkman, the Trinitron television system and the camcorder system Video 8. No wonder the company is said to be number one in the home electronics market in the U.K. The inventors in Japan keep coming up with exciting new ideas all the time: the smallest Walkman in the world, the largest TV set in the world, the smallest digital dictating machine, the lightest camcorder, and so on.

However, in the home video field it looked for a long time as though Sony might have problems. They seemed to make a mistake in their efforts to get in on the world success of video. The reason was their own Beta video system, which came on the market before VHS, and did not make it due to an unfortunate licensing strategy that became a financial and political disaster. But the staff around the company founder, Akio Morita, the genius behind the Sony brand, were not to be defeated. With his attitude of looking at the world with the eyes of an eternal optimist, and his belief in the possibility of human perfection, Morita became instrumental in creating the special Video 8 filming system in cooperation with more than 120 companies. The compact tapes and ultra-modern recording techniques of this system made possible super-light and compact camcorders, and its victory trail began in 1985.

Sony were instrumental in developing the most commonly used camcorder format, Video 8, in conjunction with a multitude of other companies.

Many technically superb and well-designed models have since been developed, confirming Sony's competence and know-how. One advantage was - and is - the fact that Sony are able to use solutions and insights from their own professional department in the products for the amateur field, making their equipment even more perfect. The long-awaited success did not fail them: although Video 8 was the last system to enter the fight for consumer approval and market share, it is now at the top of the popularity ratings and continues to grow.

There are several reasons for this. First the system's name certainly helps to encourage 'old' movie makers to switch from Super 8 to Video 8, rather than VHS or VHS-C, especially because VHS is considered more of a television recording system. Secondly, Video 8 always had the smaller smarter cameras, for example the sensational first Handycam. Finally, the developers were always just ahead of VHS when it came to technological innovations: Video 8 excelled from the beginning with clean cuts thanks to flying erase heads (VHS has fixed heads which can cause streaking at the cutting points); the sound was FM-modulated and broadcast quality from the beginning due to the technical standard agreement (on VHS it is recorded in moderate quality on a marginal track) and, compared to VHS-C, the recording time was at least twice or three times as long.

Success was therefore clearly pre-programmed, and a generous and aggressively promoted licensing policy brought it about. The latest Sony models are further proof of the continuing fight for supremacy over the competition. At the lower end of the market is the beginner's model CCD-F 350, which automatically delivers good results because all the important functions can be used in automatic mode.

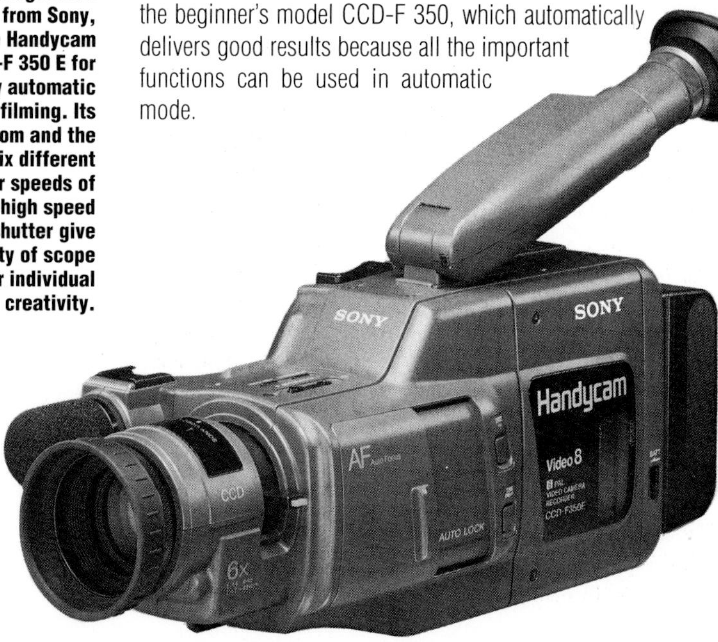

A beginner's model from Sony, the Handycam CCD-F 350 E for fully automatic video filming. Its 6x zoom and the six different shutter speeds of its high speed shutter give plenty of scope for individual creativity.

This is how it works. You simply push a panel over the controls on the side, and the camera automatically selects the aperture, white balance and focus.

Despite simple operation, it has many good features: a 6x motor zoom brings distant subjects within easy reach; a high speed shutter with six different shutter speeds reproduces even moving subjects in focus; and an impressive speed of 5 Lux allows atmospheric shots lit only by candlelight. This first-time buyer's video camera is also equipped with TTL autofocus (which can be switched on and off), a backlighting switch for fill-in light on backlit subjects, a date and time dubbing facility, a remote control attachment facility, an insert edit option (to cut new scenes into existing ones), as well as an edit search facility. This allows the operator to record over film sequences which went wrong on location, and to replace them with new sequences with minute precision. This renders superfluous the need to cut scenes later. A 1/3" CCD chip with 320,000 image elements (pixels) delivers a clear image with true colours. The image can be easily judged on the external XV-M30 LCD colour monitor which has a comfortably-sized screen 7.5cm in the diagonal.

The CCD-F 370 model goes one step further. Essentially identical to the F 350 camcorder, it has an 8x zoom, and a slightly faster 1/2" chip with a creative facility to edit in titles via a digital superimposer. In order to make things easy for first-timers, an optional starter pack includes a double battery and a filter set. A convenient bag for carrying of the camcorder and its accessories is also available. Happy shooting...

The next category of camcorder in the Sony product range impresses with easy handling and compactness. You could describe these models as compacts, but they are giants when it comes to features. There are two models; TR 45 and TR 75. These baby cameras weigh only 700g and 780g respectively and will fit into a jacket pocket, making them ideal for globetrotters. They may be small and handy but they are packed with sophisticated technical features - every millimetre is crammed full of the most modern electronics available.

The features they have in common are: digital superimposer, TTL autofocus, macro, date and time dubbing facility, edit search, record

At just 700g, Sony's CCD-TR 45E is a lightweight for problem-free video filming on the move - yet it still offers features which are missing from some larger machines.

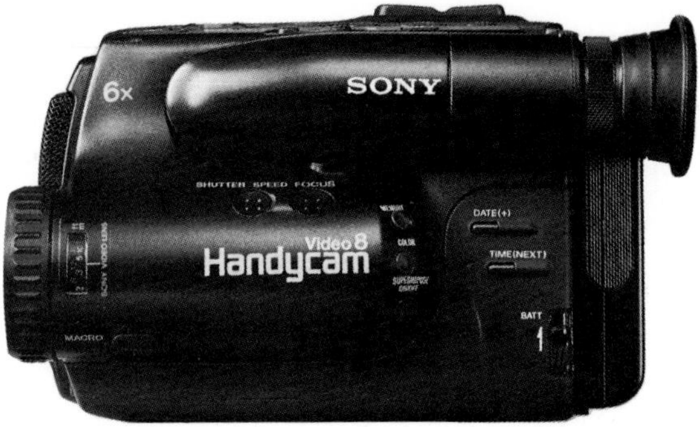

review, automatic aperture, auto white balance and six different shutter speeds between 1/50 and 1/4000 sec. The differences start in the optics: the TR 45 has a 6x zoom and a 1/3" CCD chip with 320,000 pixels; its brother, the TR 75, has an 8x zoom and a 1/2" CCD chip with 470,000 pixels, insert mode and hi-fi stereo sound. The electronic data of these two palm-size cameras are impressive, whether they're used for holiday or sports filming, as a hobby, as a professional tool, or just for fun. As their name says, they are travellers. And that stands for total mobility.

The next step up adds convenience. This category is led by the CCD-F 450, which can literally brighten up your day, for its strength lies in the dark. That is to say, its high speed delivers acceptable

Sony's CCD-TR 75 E weighs just 780g and has an 8x zoom, a CCD-chip with 470,000 pixels, hi-fi stereo sound and six different shutter speeds.

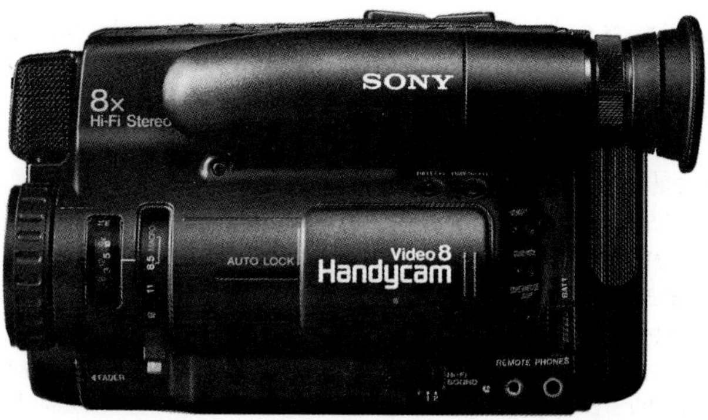

shots even at 3 (!) Lux, when other cameras have long left the viewers guessing what the picture is. Another feature is the infrared remote control in all functions, which can enable you to put yourself in the limelight. The autofocus and the 8x zoom are optical features which can give extra bite to your shots. The CCD-F 550 model offers comparable sophistication, and more: the sound is recorded in hi-fi stereo quality, with a low cut filter suppressing intrusive wind sounds. A digital superimposer with 2-page memory

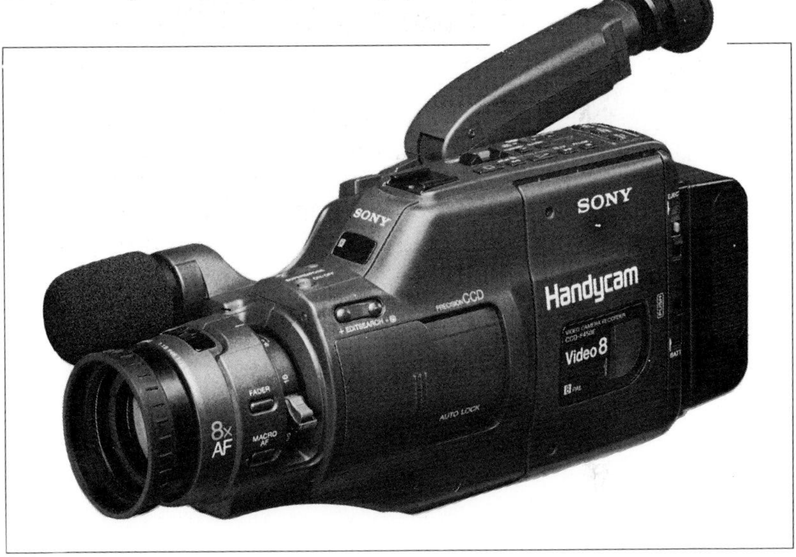

digitalises dark image details of a shot, which can then be dubbed into the running video film in one of eight colours at the press of a button. An automatic single frame transport facility (slow motion) means that the camera leaves nothing to be desired. The F 450 and F 550 pair are equipped as follows: 1/2" CCD chip with 470,000 pixels, high speed shutter with six different shutter speeds, digital superimposer, TTL autofocus, automatic TTL white balance, 3 Lux speed, date and time dubbing facility and age insert for the documentation of important events.

They also have a fader, infrared remote control, linear time counter, insert mode, record review, second record button for shots

The Sony Handycam CCD-F 450 E needs just 76 Lux for atmospheric twilight shots. An infrared remote control increases the creative possibilities.

The CCD-F 550 from Sony has hi-fi quality stereo sound, a filter to suppress wind noise and a slow motion function.

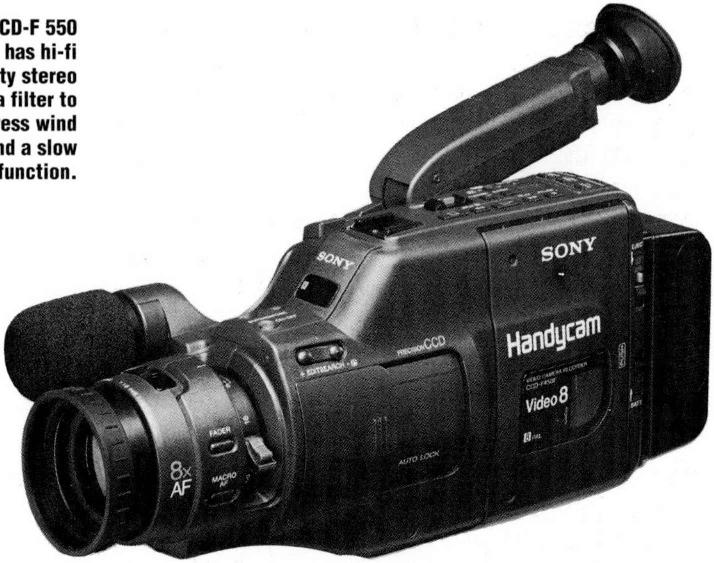

from the worm's eye view, data screen function and the facility to be connected to an editing suite, earphones and external microphone.

The CCD-V 700 model is the first in a category which surprised even professionals. It is a veritable muscleman in terms of technical sophistication, starting with its Hi-8 video system. In this system the carrier frequency of the brightness signal (luminance) is increased from 5 MHz to 7 MHz and separated from the colour information by signalling technology. Whilst Video 8 offers a horizontal resolution of approximately 250 lines, the Hi-8 system delights with a resolution of more than 400 lines. This means that video films become much sharper: plants reveal their beauty, landscape shots get even more depth and contrast, and copies suffer far less loss in quality. The electronic pre-emphasis setting also ensures that high frequency interference, which shows in the form of blurred image edges, is more effectively suppressed, and that the precision of image reproduction is increased. A special S-video output (Y/C) then guarantees that this improved signal reaches any secondary equipment, such as a monitor or VCR, without loss of quality.

But now for the brochure data of the CCD-V 700: 1/2" chip with 470,000 pixels, 8x motor zoom, high speed shutter between 1/50 and 1/10,000 sec (!) in 28 steps, digital superimposer, TTL autofocus, TTL white balance, automatic 16-stop aperture (can be switched off), 3 Lux speed, hi-fi stereo sound, date/time dubber, fader, infrared remote control, linear time counter, insert edit and single frame mode. The menu facility is also an excellent add-on. In the custom preset and picture adjust settings the image can be fine-tuned both in record and play-back mode. Colour intensity and colour tone control can therefore be adjusted according to personal taste at the point of recording. The still and slow adjust settings produce perfect still shots and automatic single frame transport without noise. An exclusive touch is added to the V 700 with the new auto manual gain system. This further intensifies, and also weakens, the signals reaching the camera computer from the chip. The result is a higher yield of signals, enabling the operator to work with faster shutter speeds even in adverse lighting conditions. In order to prevent confusion about all this technology, the camera has automatic programs which select the setting necessary for certain subject situations: first, there is a portrait mode for filming people or still life subjects; the second is a sports mode for fast-moving subjects. All in all, this is a camcorder for perfect interaction between man and technology.

The CCD-V 5000 model leads on from the V 700. This model incorporates everything Sony and video technology have to offer. This hot box, designed as a shoulder camera (weighing 3.3kg) for steady zooming and panning, has all the features which distinguish its smaller brothers: 8x motor zoom, high speed shutter, autofocus, infrared remote control, digital superimposer for creative title insertion, and so on and so forth...

But the V 5000 is a video artist of a special kind: thanks to a digital image memory device, it excels with a multitude of creative picture composition and editing features, as found in a video studio.

The digital 2x zoom allows section enlargements. A multi-picture subdivides the image into several smaller images, facilitating, for example, the analysis of movement sequences. The overlap function allows dubbing from a still image into a moving shot. All this already provides professional quality, but there is more: the picture-in-picture function enables the operator to reduce the size of a moving shot and dub it into a stored still shot. Solarization colours subjects

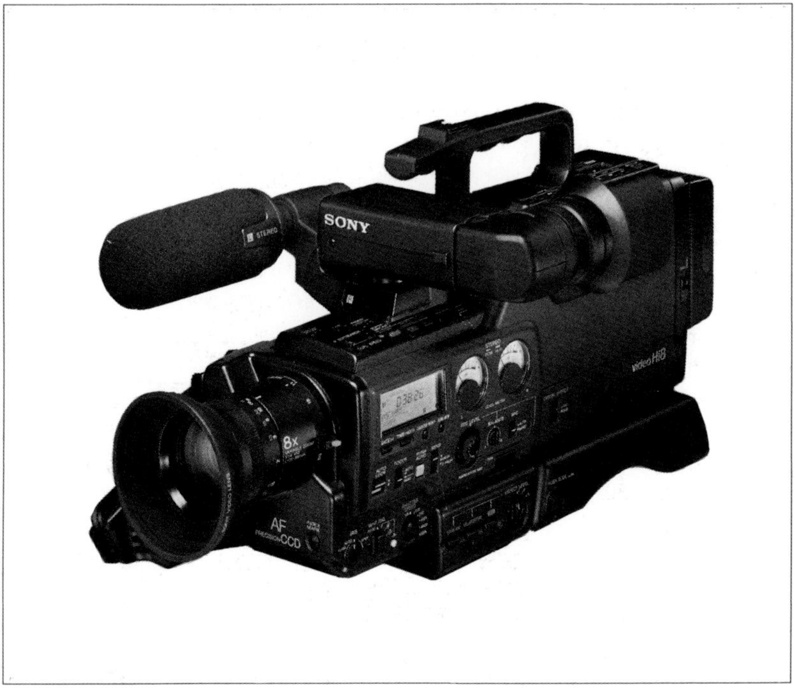

A digital image memory in Sony's CCD-V 5000 allows a multitude of creative composition and editing possibilities.

sculpturally, and the stroboscopic function offers an interesting artificial dragging effect which can be varied in three settings. This is really astonishing. Good sound quality is also built in: thanks to the Video 8-specific PCM technology used here, you can even carry out sound dubbing in outstanding hi-fi stereo quality! The sound level can be controlled either automatically or manually, and balance weighting is a further option.

A narration microphone fitted to the side of the camcorder provides the final distinction: this ensures that exciting live commentary is no longer the exclusive domain of experienced TV professionals. The camera also breaks through the barriers of the previously impossible: a $^2/3$" CCD chip with 495,000 pixels delivers a brilliant image of unsurpassed quality. The useful time base corrector levels off any mechanically-caused fluctuations in reading speed. The digital noise reduction system (DNR) automatically compensates for the noise contained in the luminance signal (black and white signal), and the speed is up to 2 Lux! All in all, Hi-8 really does make you high.

Finally, a little adventure. It is amazing what you can do with the CCD-SP 5. Thanks to its splash-proof special body, it can be used for water sports as well as a fast downhill ski-run with subjective camera; it can take a turn in tropical conditions (for example a jungle experiment in the hothouse of a botanical garden or in the real tropics) or a dusty desert excursion in adverse conditions; anything, in fact, which would get other camcorders in trouble. Externally robust, its interior accommodates a lot of sophisticated technology, at a weight of only 1,200g: five variable shutter speeds; 2-page digital superimposer for title creation, slow motion, single and still frame setting, 6x zoom with macro and autofocus. A 1/2" CCD chip with 320,000 pixels and a speed of 7 Lux capture sports subjects on video tape. Adventure calls...

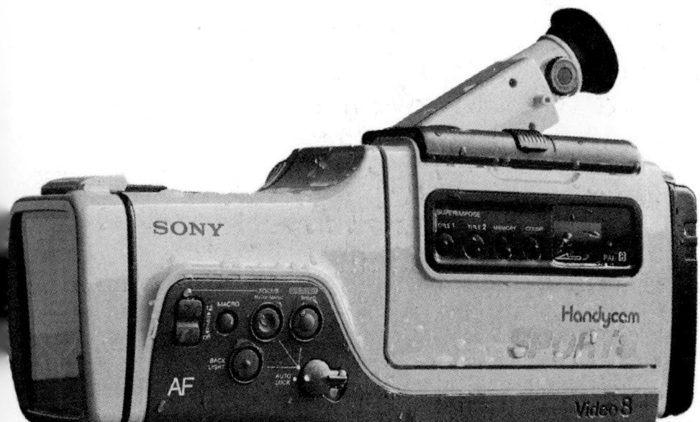

Sony's robust, splash-proof Handycam Sports CCD-SP 5 is designed for action fans. Yet it still has a generous amount of technical features.

The Systems

A knowledge of the basics is the root of understanding, and this in turn helps to avoid problems and to improve the quality of your own work.

With video, this knowledge begins with the question about the system or format used. This question already accompanied the birth pangs of the medium, and rival companies with very different methods fought over the answer to finding a way of magnetically recording television images. The different VHS and Beta systems finally emerged at the end of the 70s, and Video 2000 in the early 80s - all incompatible with each other and, apart from VHS, now no longer on the market.

Despite all this confusion, this was the big moment for private consumers who could now make video recordings at acceptable prices for the first time and then demonstrate their skills to family and friends. But the whole thing had one snag for video enthusiasts: the cameras and recorders (then running separately from the camera) were big and heavy, and video filming literally was a burden. Video film-makers were frequently met with pitying smiles by friends using their handy Super 8 movie cameras.

'Small video cassettes are a prerequisite for handy camcorders.'

The reason: a massive obstacle stood in the way of the overdue miniaturization of video cameras. The relatively large VHS, Beta and Video 2000 tapes did not allow a compact body because the tape lengths and playing times were designed for TV recording. But as generous tape lengths were not necessary for video films - a recording time of half an hour before cassette change being quite sufficient for this purpose - technicians went about the task of designing a slimmed-down version of the standard cassettes.

The results were so-called baby cassettes on VHS and Video 2000, but the latter never reached the market because the system itself was abandoned.

The former, however, became the standard system throughout the world, thanks to the victory trail of its VHS parent: VHS-C is the name for the slimmed-down VHS tape, which still has a recording time of 45 minutes and can be played on every domestic video recorder worldwide by means of a simple adaptor. The reduced dimensions of this tape (which were achieved by reducing the amount of tape in the cassette) made possible a substantial reduction of the recording mechanism and a reduction in weight.

A second development in the miniaturization of cassettes began in the early 80s under the name Video 8. It was a completely new recording method which was incompatible with the VHS method. The name was chosen for two reasons: first, because the width of the video tape was 8mm, and second because the manufacturers wanted to encourage the 'old' Super 8 movie enthusiasts to switch over to the similar-sounding video films.

To round off this small system history we need to mention that Beta did not have a go at miniaturization. For two reasons: for a start their cassette was already relatively compact - smaller than VHS and therefore more suitable for the production of camcorders; and then, the Beta format had suffered growing pains from the very beginning, and it was decided that these difficulties should not be increased by the creation a sub-system whilst the market for video filming was still in its infancy in terms of sales figures. However, the Japanese will leave nothing untried. At least one camcorder with the standard Beta cassette was therefore introduced: the Betamovie which became the first of its kind worldwide. But it made no difference - by the mid-80s the Beta star had burnt out, and VHS had become the winner in the system war.

However, a further triumphant advance was on the horizon. The small Video 8 and VHS-C cassettes, and the substitution of the bulky recording tube with a modern CCD image conversion chip, enabled the camera and recorder to be combined in one body. The ultra-compact camcorders which could be built with this system meant that video filming was no longer a feat of strength. The introduction of the Video 8 camcorder in 1985 rang in the birth of a new hobby. And there was no question who had built the camera: Sony.

Video 8

If you invent things, you also have to set standards. Sony created this basis for success by developing a total video system - Video 8 - which resulted from an agreement between 120 companies, and which, unlike all other systems, took advantage of the latest technological developments. As the system with the smallest cassette it was destined to appeal to the mobile personal video market, but it was equally suitable to become the home video system. The results were, and are, camcorders ranging between ultra-light and technically perfect with all possible features, as well as domestic recorders which are in no way inferior to their VHS system counterparts.

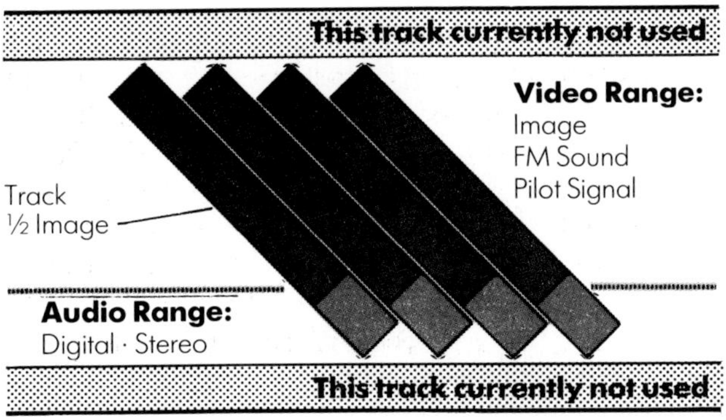

The schematic drawing explains the composition of the different tracks of a video recording.

Key to this huge market success is the fact that the so-called congenital defects of established video systems were consciously eliminated. At the centre of Video 8 is a perfected recording technique, which allows the use of ultra-compact cassettes. The main advantage of the Video 8 system lies in its extremely compact cameras with plenty of technology in the smallest possible space. If you think that the mini-tapes can only accommodate a small amount of tape material, you are wrong: the running time in standard play mode (SP) is 90 minutes. By halving the running speed in long play mode (LP) you can double the running time! So it's a great idea.

However, the quality of sound was also improved with Video 8. Whereas VHS and VHS-C cameras only record sound in reasonable quality on a modest marginal track, Video 8 records it with the video track in outstanding quality. However, by linking sound and image information, the tape cannot be audio-dubbed separately; this is only possible on a new recording, by mixing it in while recording over, or with a camcorder with extra PCM sound. The CCD-V 5000 camcorder offers this extra feature; it uses a narrow track at the lower end of each video track, adding the PCM sound information in stereo in excellent hi-fi quality at this point. As the sound can run spatially separate from the video information, the tape sound can be dubbed on afterwards. This is Video 8 in perfection, with extra space for good sound.

Hi-8

Competition livens up business; demands and encourages progress. This is why the technological lead of the Video 8 system did not let its system rival - VHS-C - rest, and the aging recording method was finally improved with the invention of Super VHS in 1987. But the lead didn't last long: Sony and other firms from the Video 8 camp countered with an identical method of image improvement - Hi-8.

Video film-makers in particular profited from this drive for quality: they had been forced to make do with simple technology for years because video had originally only been invented for time-shift recording and reproduction of television programmes.

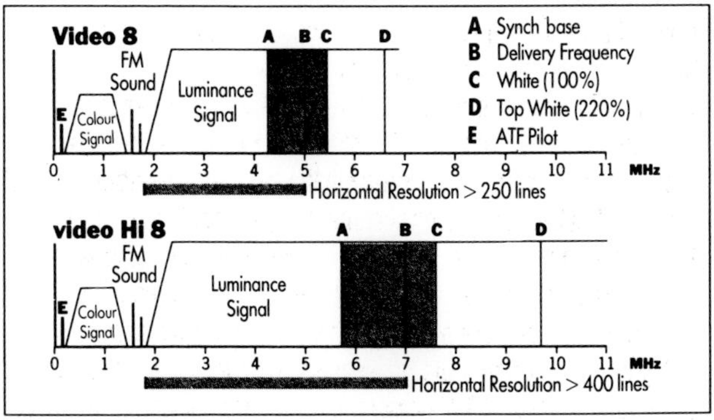

A diagram of the different frequency curves of Video 8 and Video Hi-8 recordings.

Filming, editing and copying had not been anticipated and were only made possible by the outstanding system quality of S-VHS and Hi-8. This is how they work. In the conventional VHS and Video 8 systems the recorded signals of brightness and colour (the two components which make up the image) overlap on the video tape. The advantage of this is that the data is compressed and takes up little room in the frequency spectrum. The disadvantage is that they interfere with each other and therefore reduce the sharpness the overall system can deliver. Hi-8 and Super VHS work differently: the image components brightness and colour are spatially separated when recorded in the frequency spectrum. This substantially increases resolution and sharpness performance.

The images do indeed seem more three-dimensional, intrusive colour fringing is almost completely eliminated, and the loss of quality when editing the tape by over-recording is noticeably reduced. The only snags are that films made with the Hi-8 or Super VHS systems cannot be played on conventional video recorders, and that special tapes (Metal-E for Hi-8) are needed to make full use of the quality potential - and those aren't cheap. However, experts agree that these systems represent an improvement of video recording which compares favourably with professional quality equipment, at far lower prices.

The Tapes

The stuff which video dreams are made of is a black powder, mixed together in the production of video tapes in such secrecy as if it were to be used for some secret service. Bonded to wafer-thin foil, less than a thousandth of a millimetre thick and packed into a sturdy case under sterile conditions, it stores an amazing amount of data. What we're talking about is the simple video tape, the key element in every video recording.

One thing is quite clear: a camcorder can only reach maximum performance with the right tape material! And the differences in quality between different brands become noticeable when it comes to editing and copying, if not before. A little extra money paid out can make a world of difference in image quality. This is the wrong place to try saving money.

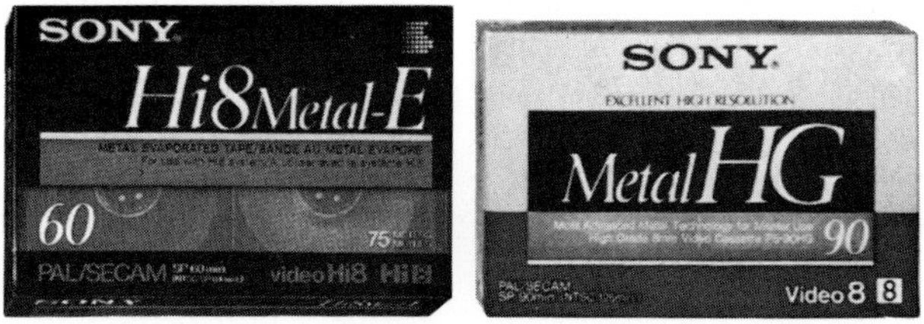

The camcorder can only provide top performance with high-quality tape material.

Last but not least, the new Hi-8 camcorders are only mediocre when used without the specially developed tape material to go with them! A considerable proportion of the extra quality is provided by the new ME (Metal Evaporated) material, which has superfine magnetic particles and a higher magnetisation capacity. The camcorder recognizes these tapes by a special code and automatically switches to Hi-8 operation. This material is necessary because the separate recording of brightness and colour requires the use of higher frequencies. This in turn means that the wavelength is shorter, and the magnetic particles therefore need to be smaller. The normal MP (Metal Powder) tapes do are not so good at fulfilling these requirements.

What's What on a Camcorder?

Admittedly, many people find it hard to grasp the vast amount that is packed into a camcorder, let alone understand the many buttons and innovations. The latter keep coming thick and fast, leaving the consumer little time to keep up. But the many creative possibilities of the camcorder can only be fully exploited if you know most or all of these things. So the most important question is: how does it all work? And, of course, what does each of these features actually do?

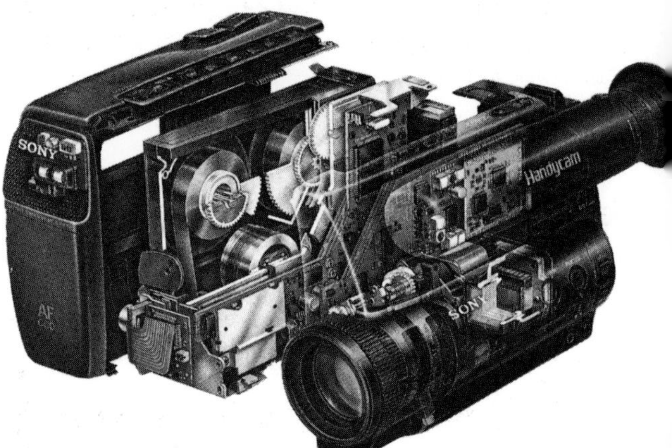

This illustration shows how much technology is accommodated inside the tiny TR Handycam from Sony.

The following section about the most important features is designed to put an end to guesswork, and to help you work with your camcorder to create superb video films. Therefore you need to know your equipment inside out.

The Viewfinder

This much is clear: whatever you see in the mini-picture tube of the camcorder viewfinder is going to be recorded. It shows what is being filmed in terms of sharpness, image section and brightness.

But that isn't all, the preview facility of the camcorder allows you to play back your recording immediately, though only in black and white for reasons of size and weight. The question whether you're overdoing it in terms of colour will therefore have to be answered by a separate colour control monitor (such as the XV-M 30), or ultimately by your television screen.

Apart from these control functions, however, the Sony technicians managed to cram quite a few other things into these compacts. You will find, for example, information about the date, the selected high speed shutter speed for exciting sports shots, the operating state of the mechanism (stop, record and so on), film title, the selected running speed (LP or SP), and much more besides.

The viewfinders of Sony camcorders are crammed full of data, and it is here that recording decisions are made. The result will show the expertise and technical ability of the film-maker.

The Lens

The interior of a lens consists of glass ground to highly sophisticated specifications, arranged in a complex sequence of specially formed elements. Allowing the selection of wide-angle to close-up settings by way of a zoom, the lens is the first link in the image recording chain - a very important part of the camera deserving protection and care.

If you are interested in the exciting world of insects and plants and want to capture it on film, you will be delighted with the macro autofocus system Sony has included with all its camcorders. With this device you will get fascinating shots in the macro range from a subject distance of approximately 10mm. Another treat is the macro autofocus device on the CCD-F 450 and CCD-F 550 models. These make filming even simpler, with the camera automatically switching to close-up range when the Macro AF button is pressed. Manual focus adjustment with the zoom lever becomes superfluous.

Camcorders without an integral macro function can be adapted for macro use with a close-up lens. An extra advantage, compared to integral macro, is that the zoom effect can be used partially!

The macro function of the autofocus control enables fascinating close-up shots of small objects.

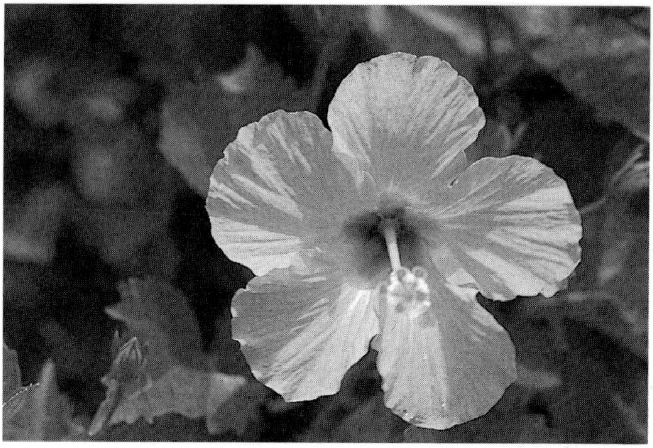

And there's more: every video film-maker will quickly notice that focusing is more critical in the telephoto range than in the wide-angle range. It is always advisable to focus in the telephoto range first before selecting the desired image section with the zoom. That's how the professionals do it!

The Autofocus

Everybody knows that automatic functions are great, but they're even better when they can be switched off. Sony fulfil this wish in all their camcorders, because there will always be situations when you would like a less than sharp image; for example to indicate dream sequences, or to have one scene end in soft focus with the next one starting the same way. This is an elegant technique for describing and expressing changes of time or location.

Sometimes automation simply doesn't know how to select the desired detail from a variety of image information. A press of the button is all that's required to put you in control of the image, and to allow you to add the highlights to your film.

The Image Sensor

Fragile as an eggshell, the recording chip is located behind the optical system, registering everything that happens in front of the camera. But despite the thick wall of glass in front of it, the camera's eye is in danger: its main enemy is strong direct light which can destroy its delicate sensor pixels. This is why you should never film into blazing light with your camcorder. The rule of thumb is that a light source you can still look at with the naked eye will not damage the image sensor.

A little bit of technical information clarifies the sophistication of this delicate centre piece. Its correct name is CCD - Charge Coupled Device. It consists of a chip smaller than a finger nail and has very quickly replaced the good old recording tube. Its strength lies in the fact that it has drastically reduced the power consumption, weight and dimensions of camcorders. It has the same task as its predecessor, the picture tube: to convert light - that is the image fixed in the lens - into electronic signals, which can then be recorded onto the magnetic tape.

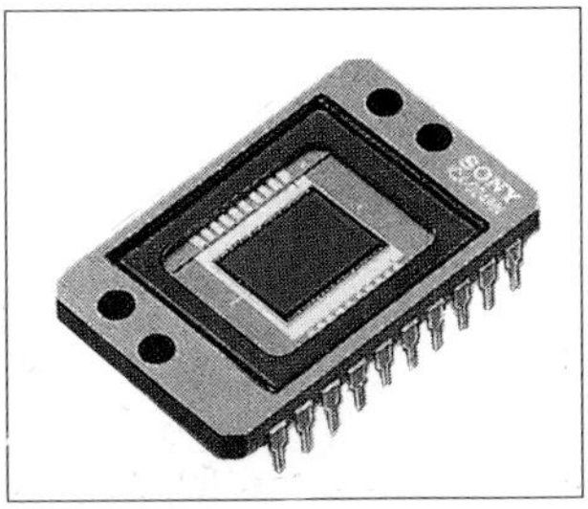

The tiny high-resolution CCD-chip, the electronic eye of Sony's camcorders, is a real masterpiece of technology in the smallest possible space.

What does this look like? Such a chip consists of tiny image elements, so-called pixels, arranged in the shape of a grid. There is an amazing number of these: for example, up to 495,000 (!) of them are found on an area of $^{2}/3$" in the CCD-V5000 camcorder - hence also the name $^{2}/3$" CCD chip. When light falls onto these elements, every pixel immediately produces a voltage, which corresponds to the colour and brightness data and is fed into the electronic system of the camera and the recorder. The result is the video signal.

One more point: for technical reasons not all of these pixels can be used to build the image; some of them have to serve other purposes. We have to distinguish between gross and net pixels, and a comparison of chip performance should only ever take into account the numbers of active pixels.

Naturally, the sophisticated Hi-8 method uses chips with higher pixel numbers than Video 8 because the camera can only record what is registered as image information. Sony have gone one step further towards increased sharpness and precision of detail on the F 450, F 550, F 700 and TR 75 models; moreover, they have also improved the chip filter: the image converters of these models use a complementary matrix colour filter technique consisting of the complementary colours cyan, yellow and magenta, and the primary colour green. This ensures brilliant video results, and it is, after all, better to be on the safe side...

The Exposure Control System

Rules prevent chaos. They also ensure that everything is balanced - even in a camcorder. Nothing must be too loud or too quiet, too bright or too dark. In order to free the film-maker from these problems, they are taken over by automatic programs. Like the iris of the human eye, the aperture control system regulates the intensity of the light reaching the image chip. This is necessary because the image chip only has a narrow range of sensitivity, so the exposure control system has to take on the job of adapting the amount of light to the CCD chip. The principle is simple: the brighter the light, the more the aperture is narrowed, and vice versa. Light in its many nuances is a fascinating, but complicated subject, requiring a lot of technical know-how if it is to be used and recorded in a way which is natural and true to life. Correct exposure is essential for good shots.

'Like the iris of the human eye, the exposure control system regulates the intensity of the light entering the camera.'

If you still prefer to rely on your own eyes, or if you want to achieve unusual effects, the Sony V 700 and V 5000 camcorders will give you the opportunity to override the automatic system with a manual option. Again, the best automatic system is one that can sometimes be switched off.

The Video Head

It's like being on a helter skelter. The video head converts the electric signals into magnetic data at a breakneck rotation speed. It is, as it were, the stenographer of the camera.

But it's not as easy as it sounds because physical laws have presented the technicians with a few tough nuts to crack: the extremely high frequency spectrum of video data represents a large amount of data which would require an extremely large amount of tape material to be recorded. The inventors of video recording therefore used a trick: instead of a high tape speed requiring a correspondingly large amount of tape, they chose a high recording speed which is achieved by video heads rotating at very high speed. A second step towards reducing the amount of tape required was the extreme reduction of the magnetic tracks: they are just 0.049mm wide! These tracks are written by tiny heads on the head drum; only 0.5 micrometres wide, they are made from very fine crystalline ferrous material. At 1,500 revolutions per minute, these heads rotate and race across the video tape which is wound around the head

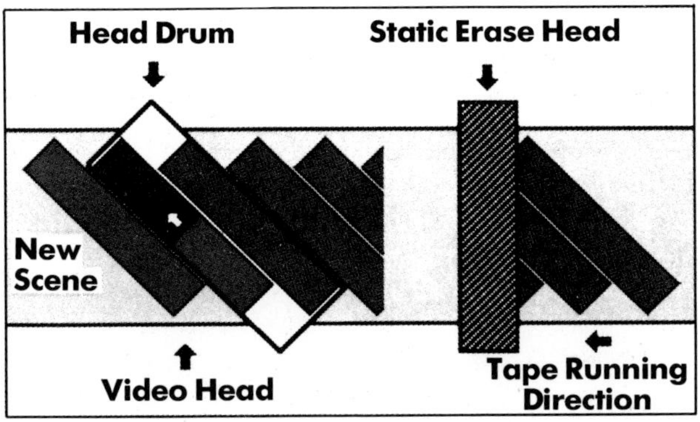

This schematic diagram of the start of a new scene shows how much sophisticated technology is required for a video recording.

drum, thereby completing the recording and reproduction cycle.

Talking of recording: all old data does have to be erased beforehand. This is done by a special erase head which is also located on the rotating head drum; it is synchronised with the writing and reading heads and therefore ensures that scenes are linked together cleanly.

One last tip: due to the high speed of the head drum, the air circulation resulting from it and the inevitable tape friction, this component in particular is a dust and dirt trap. Regular maintenance of the valuable camera is especially advisable if you work in hostile conditions (dust, smoky rooms and so on). Service agents will professionally clean tape tracks, head drum and video heads. Sony camcorders will reward regular maintenance with constant outstanding image quality and reliable operation.

The Mechanism

Things work as if by magic in the cassette compartment: the video is automatically threaded; careful grips wind it around the head drum to be read; at the same time the tape transport motor is set into motion, and the head drum with the video heads accelerates as if it is trying to set a new speed record.

A split second later an air cushion is formed between the head drum and the video tape in order to avoid the wafer-thin magnetic tape being ripped by the drum, which is by now rotating at a speed of 1,500 revolutions per minute. And then the camcorder is ready to shoot again.

What we're talking about is the machine room, the mechanism of the camcorder which carries out those humble mechanical jobs

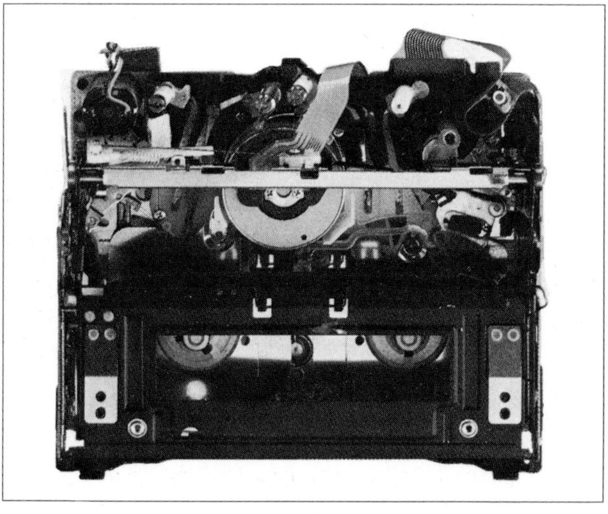

The tiny mechanism of the Handycam TR camcorder from Sony is a perfect example of miniaturization and the integration of fine mechanics and electronics.

which allow you to capture reality on tape. The miniature mechanism of the TR 45 in particular, with its amazing weight of 700g, is a prime example of miniaturization which only seems to be limited by minimum ergonomic requirements.

However, this also means that foreign particles must never be allowed to get into the cassette compartment! You can only ensure that the Sony camcorder will function properly by taking very good care of it.

The Microphone

It's not what you say but the way you say it - or in this case the way you hear it! Everybody knows that, including the video film-maker. The original sound of a recording is particularly important because it conveys the acoustic mood.

The superior high quality Video 8 technology of Sony's stereo camcorders, such as the V 700, F 550 and TR 75 models, have the right qualifications for the job. The V 5000 model takes the lead in this area; it records sound on a separate PCM track in hi-fi stereo quality, paving the way for creative audio dubbing! This option makes sense if you want to replace unusable sound passages, dub original scenes with music or commentary, or emphasise dramatic incidents by adding acoustic effects.

All Sony camcorders have connections for additional microphones if the high quality integral Electret condenser microphone is to be switched off for some reason. This can be useful if a different choice of microphone could be more suitable for certain situations: for example a clip-on microphone for interviews, or a directional microphone for distant subjects.

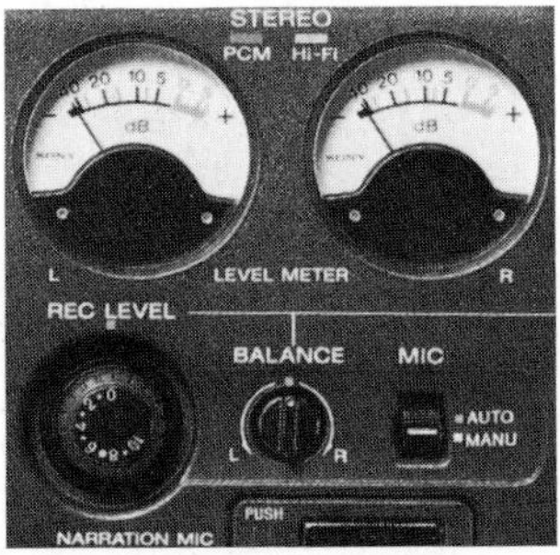

The hi-fi stereo sound recorded on a separate PCM track can be balanced precisely on the Sony V-5000.

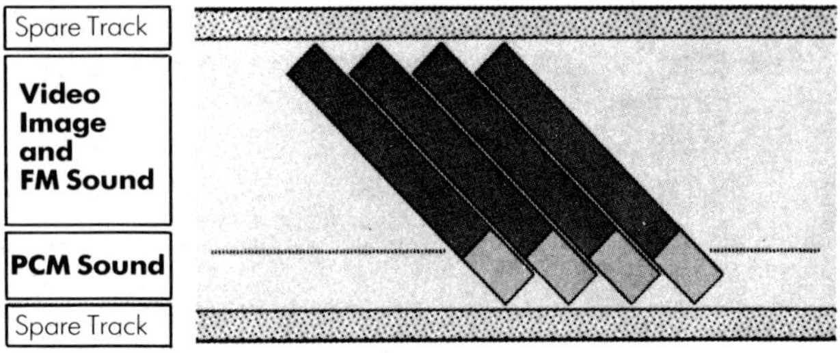

The schematic diagram shows the track distribution for video image and FM as well as PCM sound of Video 8 video tapes.

A snappy soundtrack can be created with an audio mixer. Two additional sources of sound can be plugged into its microphone socket for sound to be fed in and mixed. So you could please your audience's ears as well as their eyes by using a Walkman to dub *The Moonlight Sonata* onto a video of a sunset.

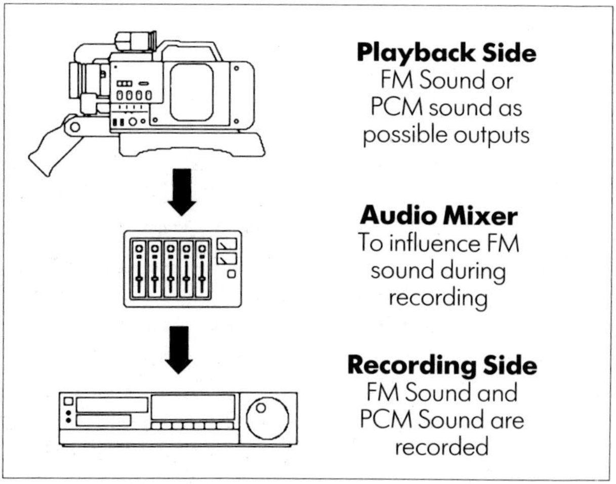

Professional audio mixers allow sound recording and playback via separate PCM and FM tracks. Whereas the FM sound signal is mixed into the image signal, PCM sound uses a separate track.

By Hand or with Tripod

The smaller the camcorder, the more tempting it is to film with it hand-held. After all, that's the whole point of miniaturization. But you should remember that even the lightest camcorders have zooms with a six to eight times focal length range, whose maximum telephoto focal length corresponds to one of 300mm or more in the 35mm camera format. The longer the focal length used, the higher the danger of camera shake. Photographers using 35mm film hardly ever take pictures hand-held with such long telephoto lenses, not even sports photographers. So what applies to the 35mm photographer can be applied to video filming: Here, too, a steady camera is the be-all and end-all. It decides whether your viewers will get uncomfortable after just a few minutes of watching the video, or whether they can relax and enjoy it.

In order to hold the camcorder as steady as possible, you should stand with your legs apart, firmly pressing the camcorder against your face and shoulder, and your arms against your chest. If you are following a subject with the camera, you should turn your entire upper body whilst your legs remain firmly planted on the ground.

A Small Prop

Whenever you have the chance, you should always lean against, or rest on, something when filming with the camcorder hand-held. A tree, a lamp-post, a car, a door frame or the wall of a house can contribute substantially to the quality of your recordings.

You can even improve the image quality by resting on the back of a chair or the top of a table.

Small irregularities of movement are less conspicuous in recordings of moving subjects than of static ones. If the viewer knows that the subject is still, every jolt appears doubly unnatural.

If you are walking with the camera, it is best to move sideways. You should choose a movement similar to the cross-over step in ice skating, where the free leg moves past the other one to the front whilst the upper body remains steady. Try to avoid zooming whilst panning or moving with the camcorder - it would only make the picture unsteady.

Shoulder Stocks

Shoulder stocks and monopods are available as accessories and are useful aids for filming as they allow a lot of freedom of movement. They are relatively light and don't take up as much room as a video tripod.

Shoulder stocks don't just contribute to a steadier camera position, they also ensure a better distribution of the camera's weight, leading to better video recordings without a lot of extra strain. At the same time, the better distribution of weight and additional support help prevent you getting tired quickly.

A number of quite different types of stocks are on offer for hand-held work. Some very light ones really are only shoulder stocks, others are more elaborate and may be used as a small tripod, for example. Shoulder stocks have a supporting surface which easily adjusts to the shape of the shoulder. The length of the stock can be individually adjusted with the telescopic tube.

An integral supporting plate serves for attaching the camcorder, and its angle can be adjusted depending on the recording situation. Many shoulder stocks are small and handy, ideal for mini-

A camcorder shoulder stock allows a lot of freedom of movement.

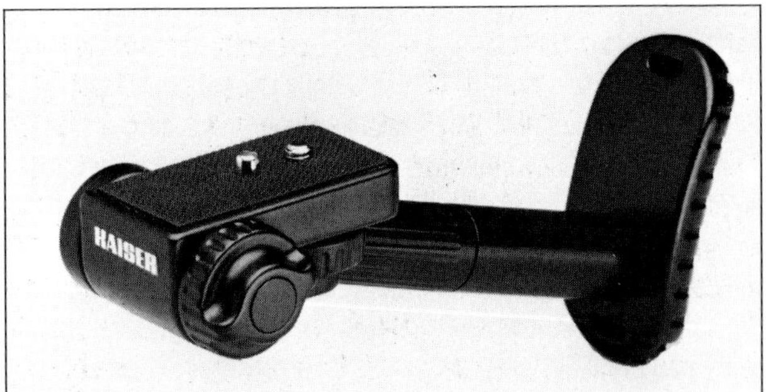

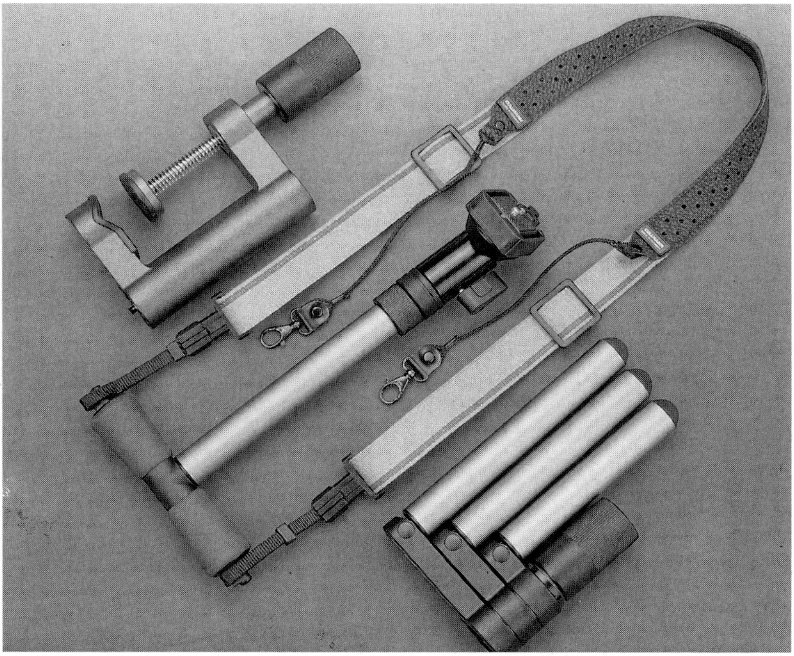

camcorders. Most can stay on the camcorder permanently, and can be folded to the base of the camcorder for transport. But although they can substantially reduce mistakes, they cannot guarantee shake- or jolt-free work.

A clip-on stock, a miniature version of a table stock and a body/chest stock.

More suitable for suppressing typical filming shake are so-called chest stocks with shoulder straps. These stocks have a strap which goes around the neck, and the stock itself is attached to the strap at stomach height. Chest stocks are available from good accessory companies. The Novoflex stock can be used as both a shoulder and a chest stock.

The Cullman chest stock has two additional support straps which can be attached to the stock head. This means that you can let go of the camcorder between recordings without it falling down. The advantage of both these devices is their relatively low weight and compact construction.

Monopods

Monopods do allow a steadier camera position than shoulder stocks, but they also restrict the video film-maker's freedom of movement. They are ideally suited as supports during zooming and panning, but the film-maker cannot change the shooting position during recording. Their special advantage obviously lies in their low weight and quick set-up. Many video film-makers leave unextended monopods dangling from the camcorder permanently, or have fitted them with a quick release device whose coupling plate stays attached to the camcorder. There are also sturdy tripods whose centre leg can be taken out and turned into a practical monopod with head and quick coupling device.

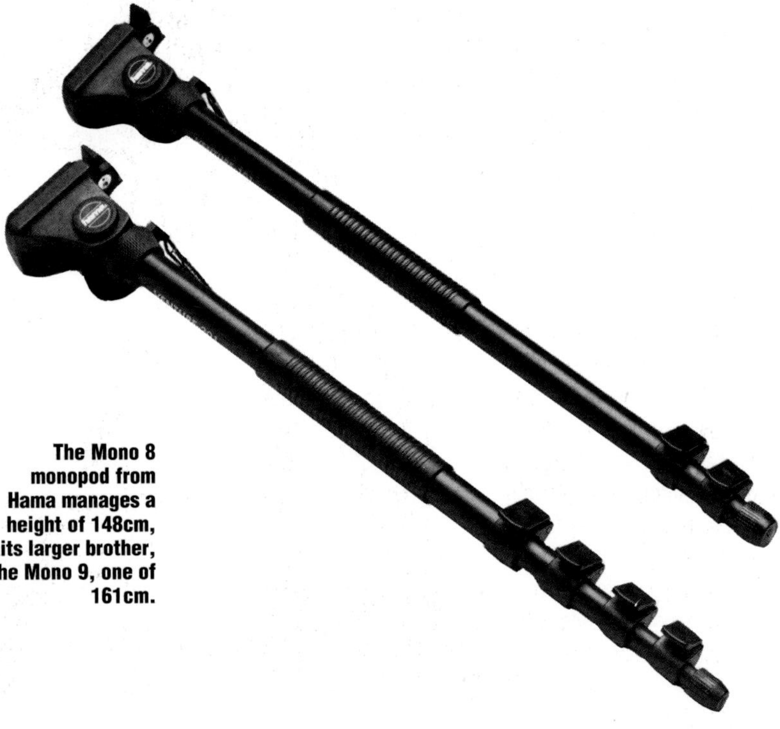

The Mono 8 monopod from Hama manages a height of 148cm, its larger brother, the Mono 9, one of 161cm.

Video Tripods

Anyone using a tripod makes the highest demands of their recordings, and is therefore even prepared to put up with the setting up and the inconvenient carrying around that comes with it. One tip right at the start: the sturdier a tripod, the higher the likelihood of getting really shake-free recordings. Tripods aren't just important for jolt-free panning, steady zooming and shake-free recordings, they are also necessary for exact working, precisely determining image sections and to ensure steady image tracking. Video films recorded using the long focal length setting of the lens produced exclusively with a hand-held camcorder, or even with a shoulder stock, will always be unsteady. The longer the focal length, the larger the reproduction ratio, and the slightest jolt or movement will appear all the more annoying on the television monitor later. Distance and close-up shots should never be taken without a sturdy tripod.

A video film-maker is served well with a quality tripod with an integral monopod.

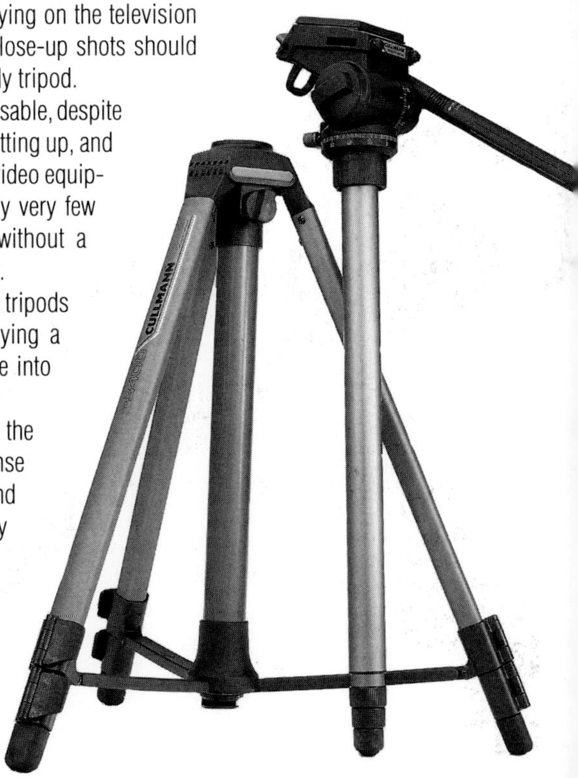

Using a tripod is always advisable, despite the preparation required for setting up, and the extra weight added to the video equipment. There are probably only very few creative reasons for doing without a camcorder support altogether.

The range of available video tripods is almost endless. When buying a tripod you should always take into account a number of factors:

- Although sturdiness is the main concern, it makes no sense to buy a tripod whose size and weight mean that it will usually be left at home.
- The video tripod should be quick and easy to set up. This means that it needs to have simple, easily operated clamps to lock the height of the legs.

● If possible it should have an adjustable centre column because once the tripod is set up, its height is more easily adjusted than that of the three legs. (Some centre columns can also be used as monopods.)

● A spirit level on the tripod head is useful for the exact alignment of the camcorder on the tripod, for example for architectural shots.

● The maximum extension height of the tripod is not the only important concern. How far down you can go for shots from the worm's eye view could also make a difference.

● Central struts between the legs of particularly light video tripods can give extra sturdiness and more stability.

The Tripod Head

The tripod head has a decisive influence on the quality of your video recordings. On the one hand it serves for the attachment of the camcorder and should enable the smoothest possible horizontal and vertical panning. You need to be able to lock the camcorder in position along both directional tracks, quickly and separately. You should make sure that your tripod head has a suspension spring for vertical adjustment so that the camcorder does not tip down when you let go of it. An integral spirit level for the exact alignment of the camcorder is almost indispensable, to make sure, for example, that the horizon really is horizontal in your shot.

You should also pay particular attention to the tilt arm of the tripod head. It points backwards on most tripods and can at most be adjusted slightly in its angle. A tilt arm pointing backwards between camera and video film-maker rather gets in the way on small camcorders. Some tripods have adjustable tilt arms or handles, which can point either to the front or the back.

The quick release device also deserves attention. On smaller camcorder models in particular, it is important that the width of the coupling plate roughly corresponds to that of the camera base.

It should stay on the camcorder in order to facilitate fast, easy switching between hand-held and tripod recording.

An additional feature of good tripod heads is the facility to attach accessory tracks for lamps or external microphones.

Tripod Dollies

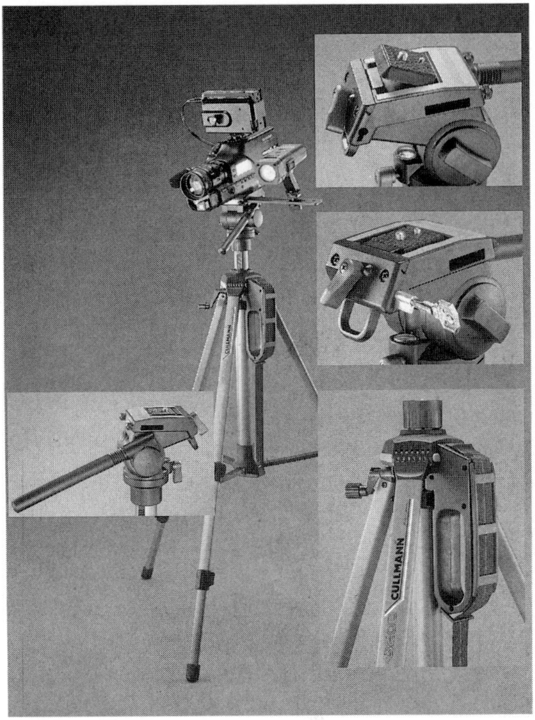

Collapsible dollies are available as accessories with many tripods. However, an absolutely smooth surface is necessary for successful dollying, otherwise the recording quality is reduced by shaking and jolting. Professionals often even build tracks for dollying. Indoors a smooth parquet or linoleum floor is best suited for amateur dollies.

Special tripods for video filming from the car are readily available. A popular model is a monopod combined with suction feet. The three segments of the monopod are locked at the desired height with stretch clips. A video head with quick release device for vertical panning is built-in. The monopod is firmly anchored between the front and the side window with the help of a support strut unit with suction feet; this unit can be extended by an angle of 90°, and its length can also be adjusted by means of stretch clips.

Tripod heads, available in different types from normal to fluid, are vital for serious video filmmakers using a tripod.

A polarising filter should always be used when filming through car windows in order to avoid intrusive reflections. Such filters are available from quality photo and video dealers.

Repro Stands and Recording Tables

Special stands are available for close-up shots and reproductions. A macro repro stand is particularly versatile; it is suitable for video

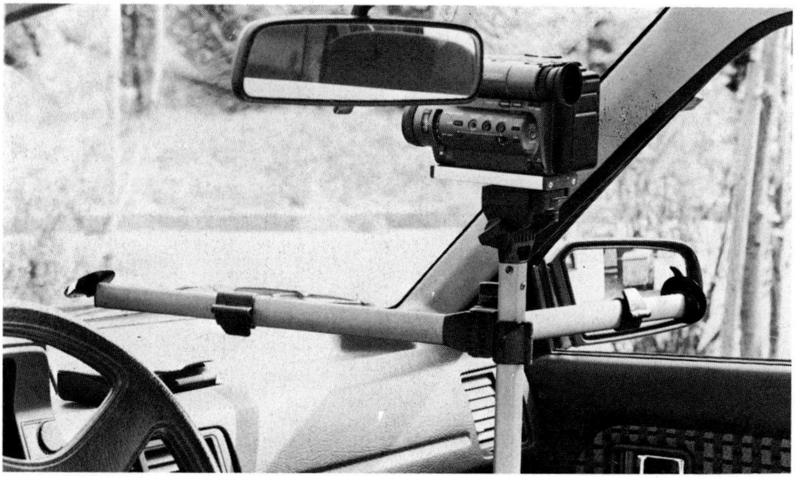

Special car stocks are available for video filming from the car.

recordings of small subjects, as well as the transfer of slides or negatives onto video. The possibility to attach video lamps, which can be positioned perfectly by means of so-called swans' necks, is a further practical feature of this stand. Repro tables are ideal for dedicated repro work. Whereas the repro stands have an integral support for the camcorder, an additional sturdy video tripod is required for working on the recording table.

From Idea to Script

If you go out with your video camera and film everything totally at random you are going to do one of two things - bore your audience or give yourself a substantial amount of work at a later date editing.

A simple way of seeing this literally is to go out and shoot whatever is in front of you, come home and play it back through your TV - you will realise you have a jumble of miscellaneous material with perhaps hopefully some outstanding items here and there.

Think before you shoot - sit down and plan out your video filming, with the actual end product you want to present to your audience uppermost in your mind.

Just remember boring television, when the absence of anything dramatic sends you to sleep. In video filming, too, it isn't enough just to record whatever moves in front of the lens and then to simply reel it all off. Even a very few rules are enough to bring order and style into home recordings, and therefore to guarantee success.

We mustn't forget the fascinating possibilities of re-working your films after you have got your recordings in the bag. By editing with effect devices, using titles and post sound recording, you can complete and perfect your work. But the recording, and therefore the period between realising the first idea and the script, comes before everything else.

Thinking

Whether you carry out your thinking in the bath, or walking the dog, it doesn't matter, but at the end of the day the clear message is the same - think before pressing the button!

So how can you at least encourage creativc film ideas? Two methods have proven very useful:

1. Freewheeling - letting thoughts move freely with creative dreams.

2. Brainstorming - creating flashes of inspiration.

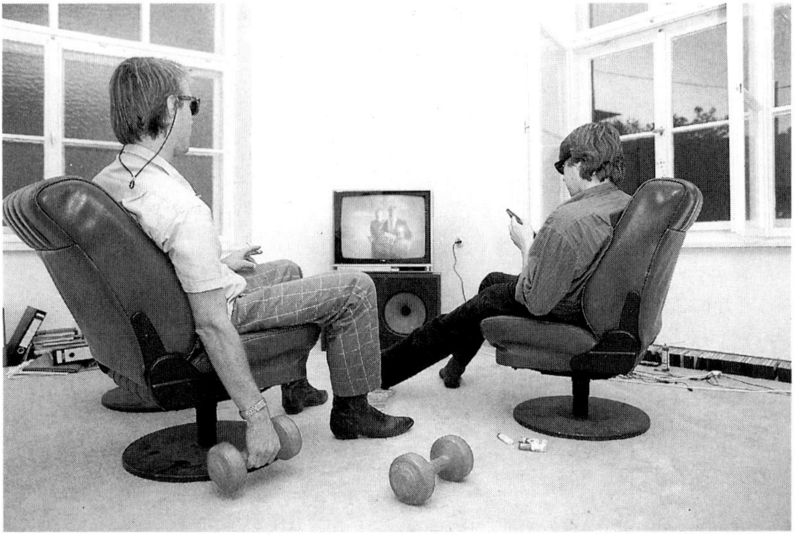

You won't make a good film without good ideas. Gather all your most creative powers to realise your video plans.

What are these techniques based on? The realisation that one idea leads to others. Freewheeling and brainstorming are based on the simple principle of thought association.

Imagine you're sitting with friends one evening. At first everything is fairly dull and conversation is a real effort. Just before everyone decides to call it a day somebody tells a joke. And then another one. Suddenly you also remember one and tell it. And all of a sudden everybody remembers one as well - the very people who had previously sat there all clammed up. Now everyone gets in the swing of it, and so the evening goes on.

This is the exact basis of both methods: one word leads to another, one thought triggers another which you would never have thought of otherwise. You can have this type of thought association, get one thought to lead to the next, even when you are alone. This is precisely what freewheeling is. Before we make a decision which is even remotely important to us, we let our thoughts wander freely and easily. It doesn't matter where, when or how.

One basic rule: write everything down! And a second one: never correct yourself straight away. We should avoid immediate judgement. Many ideas are successful precisely because they helped you do or achieve something which seemed impossible only the day before.

Eventually we will go over our brainwaves, discard the unusable and meaningless ones, until we are left with a short-list of just a few. We pick the best idea and go to work!.

You proceed in the same way for brainstorming, except that you don't produce ideas on your own, but with other people. As in freewheeling, it is important that you separate the two phases - producing the ideas and critiquing them.

Interestingly, experiments have shown that the seventieth idea is on average the best! That a little effort is worthwhile is also evidenced by the realisation that the second quarter of an hour produces two to three times as many ideas as the first. So thinking hard really is worthwhile! Freewheeling and brainstorming can also help you make more of a rainy Sunday. There are certainly more original ways of realising great video films than those suggested by camcorder brochures. So mobilise your slumbering powers, it's your film after all!

You need ideas to turn holiday scenes into a video film worth seeing, as well as for setting a birthday party or sporting event in the right atmosphere.

Basic Principles

The fruit of the creative process is the finished script, which is your interpretation of your subjective feelings in a language which can be generally understood. The small grain that was your basic idea becomes the growing crystal of a story with which you aim to captivate your audience.

There are really no universal rules for script writing, but there are a few basic principles which should be taken into account:

● Pay attention to the diversity of the stories. As in life, anything's possible.

● Pay attention to the inner strength of the story. Techniques such as chase or action scenes hold the viewer's attention and increase suspense.

● Pay attention to the dramatic build-up. Save the best bit to the end.

Scriptwriting

A scriptwriter has to offer the audience what they want, but hadn't expected. There are no rules of story-telling, but a number of principles which have worked time and time again. Accordingly, the dramatic structure of the story has the function of bringing to light the inner nature of a human being. This is done with scenes in which the protagonist is under pressure or faced with decisions - the protagonist is the emotional gateway to the story, which should have a central theme. This could be, for example: Love Triumphs, Mother Nature has the Last Word, Justice Wins, or Pride comes before a Fall. The exposition at the beginning should be powerful enough to introduce the story with a dramatic bang to gain the viewer's interest. What remains is the question: How do you actually write the script?

It's simple: from beginning to end, and at first completely without dialogue. Your efforts are only ready for the dialogue to be added when the story is complete, the story-lines spun, the highlights organised, and when the network of the subconscious and the unspoken has been created.

In technical terms, the script contains dialogues and the descriptions of the object to be filmed. Producing it is therefore not so much a creative art but rather a craft. You don't just start writing like mad, but methodically develop a film idea. Three stages of development can be distinguished:

1. The exposé
2. The treatment
3. The script.

In the exposé the main facts of the future script are determined in just a few pages. Details can be omitted, clarity and outline are the key. It is like a skeleton to which the flesh is to be added later. The treatment is an elaboration of the expose and tells the whole story, but without a detailed description of scenes. It indicates the sequence of scenes only roughly, but it can contain dialogue. This is the time for corrections, because you have the conclusive material in front of you.

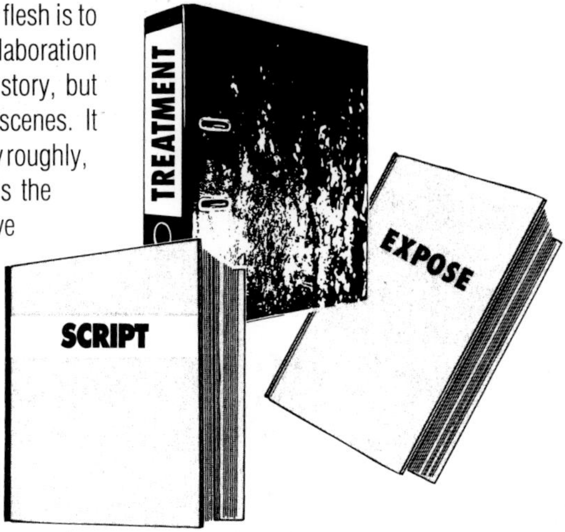

You should also take into account the internal dynamics of the story. It can happen that a story sounds completely credible in the exposé, but then becomes impossible when it is fleshed out in the treatment, requiring replacement with other events in order to stay credible. Everybody knows cinema films where initially congenial heroes become ridiculous idiots in the course of events, perhaps because the audience subconsciously transferred their sympathies to another person - even though the author did not intend that to happen.

The way out of this dilemma can be found by breaking down story elements into motives and intentions, aims or difficulties. This is achieved by a detailed analysis with a very critical eye. It is the only way of finding the good and bad qualities of your material.

The script is the final realization of your film material. It describes the film's scenes, it is a film creation manual. Like an architectural drawing which helps construction experts turn the ideas of the architect and the structural engineer into the concrete reality of a building, a good script describes the film scene by scene for the director, camerman, actors, etc.

This is how you go about it. Take a sheet of paper, divide it with a line down the middle, and fill in all the information regarding the image on the left-hand side: inside or out; day or night; close-up or distance shot; single person, group or landscape; plus timings and camera positions. All sound data goes in the right-hand column: dialogue, sound or music. The script can, of course, change during filming - nobody can predict all eventualities: actors can fall ill, you can get periods of bad weather, and often it turns out that a scene was good only on paper. Also, you shouldn't deny your creative potential if it is obvious that a story doesn't gel properly. This is the only way to avoid the dreaded dilemma many video film-makers are faced with: they work too spontaneously and arrive at the conclusion that having ideas is heavenly, but turning them into films is not so easy.

Film scenes are described in detail in the script. Sound effects and dialogue are also entered in it.

Script: Title: The visit	Author: Pit Muller
IMAGE	**SOUND**
Outside: Overall shot, street car pulls up and stops outside the door of No. 68	Original sound Sound effects
Outside: Semi-total shot of car, driver gets out, camera follows, driver approaches door	Man mumbles: "I hope somebody is at home"
Outside: Close-up shot, doorbell, hand	Door bell sound
Inside: Woman in the kitchen, cutting beans	Woman calls: "It's open, come in"

Production Planning

It costs money to make a video film. And the only way to limit your expenditure is by planning. This covers three areas: preparation, filming and re-working. The video film-maker is faced with the task of organising and developing a large number of tasks. These include working on the manuscript and the script, working out an editing plan, liaising with cast and crew, preparing for production (looking for locations, building the set), filming itself, the technical re-working of the recorded material, as well as cutting and synchronization at the final editing stage.

Production planning includes everything: coordinating materials, manpower, and time so that the project runs without problems at the right time, in the right place and with the right people.

Location

The correct location is usually determined by the film theme. You can't move a wedding to a location which is more attractive to you. If possible you should familiarise yourself with the known surroundings in advance. From what perspective will you get the best shots? Where will you find a position where people don't keep running into your shot? Perhaps you can find a way of filming events from above, in order to get bigger groups of people in the shot. Here, too, planning is everything.

The Actors

A film idea takes shape with the actors and the audience will see their own experiences reflected in the actors. Their role is therefore multi-functional, and that means completely entering the thoughts of the people whose parts they play by acting in a way that wins the audience over to the message of the film.

The actors in your films will mainly be friends and relatives. Never

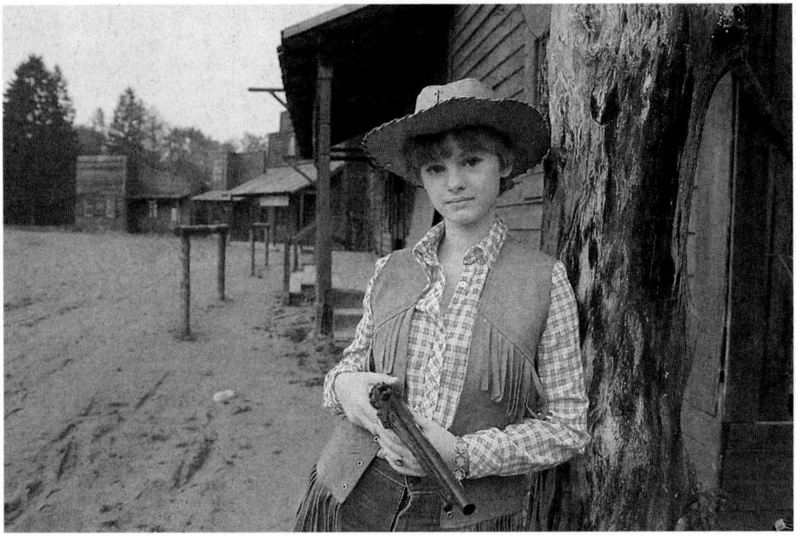

Participants find it easiest to be convincing in their parts if they can identify with them.

expect too much from their acting talents. It is an advantage if actors already have characteristic qualities of the part they are playing rather than having to put themselves in the position of a different person. This is the only way of enabling them to make the desired impression on the audience. Being natural in front of the camera is the first commandment and, unlike trained actors, amateurs find this difficult. Usually they want to present something, and this is exactly where they go wrong. Children are far better at this: their appearance in front of the camera isn't a play in which they want to put themselves on stage, but a natural expression of their way of life. They present themselves in the way they are, and that's exactly what makes for perfect acting.

Props

A film doesn't live by actors alone. Clothes and décor, set and costume details, and objects to be used - props in the widest sense of the word - form a dramatic space which gives additional definition to the cast.

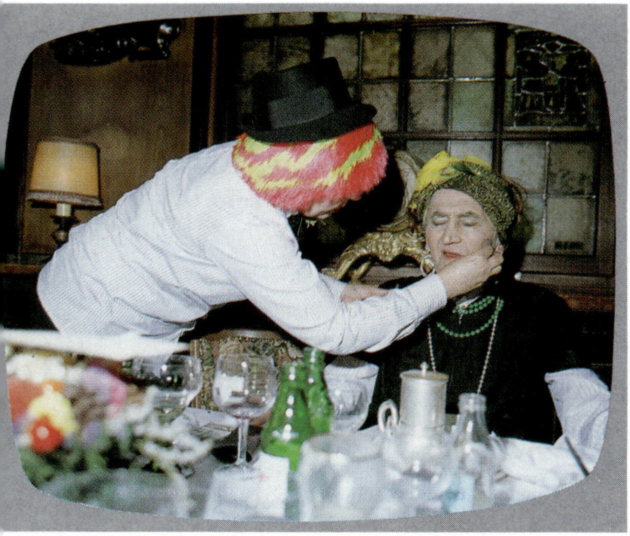

The family group: memories of family parties, whether carnival, Easter or Christmas, must be captured with the camcorder. The preparations such as make-up...

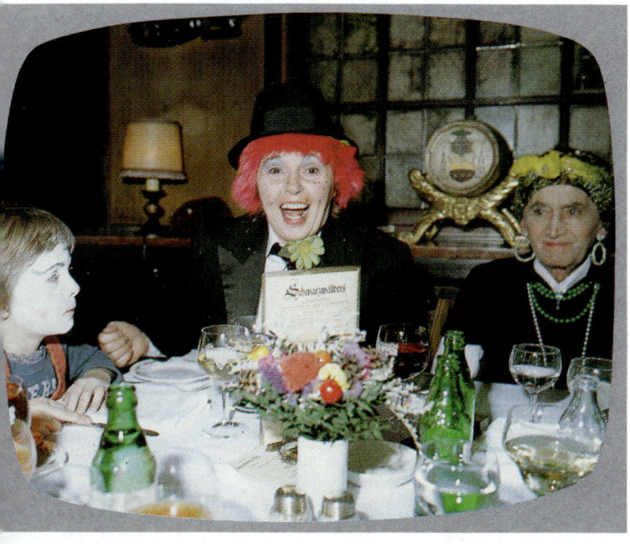

...are as much part of it as the party itself. Small episodes are turned into an entertaining feature film by editing at home.

Holiday memories: Who doesn't enjoy remembering the best days of the year? The romantic harbour scenery in the warm evening light of the Greek island...

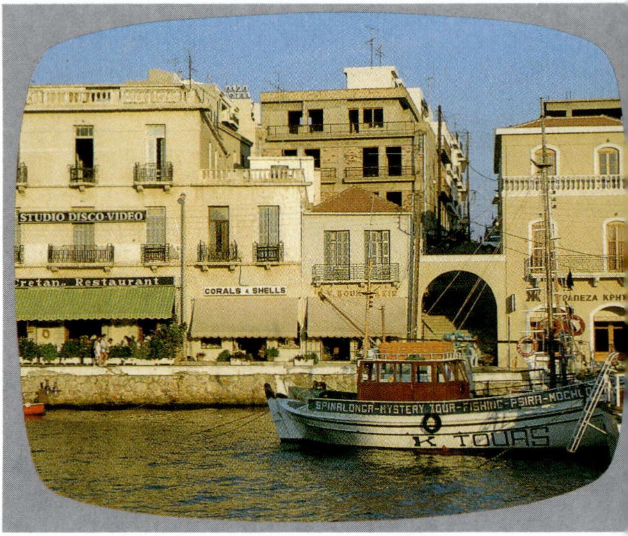

...or the fishing boats which will remind you of sea and holidays when you watch them on video later. Different perspectives will make your film more interesting.

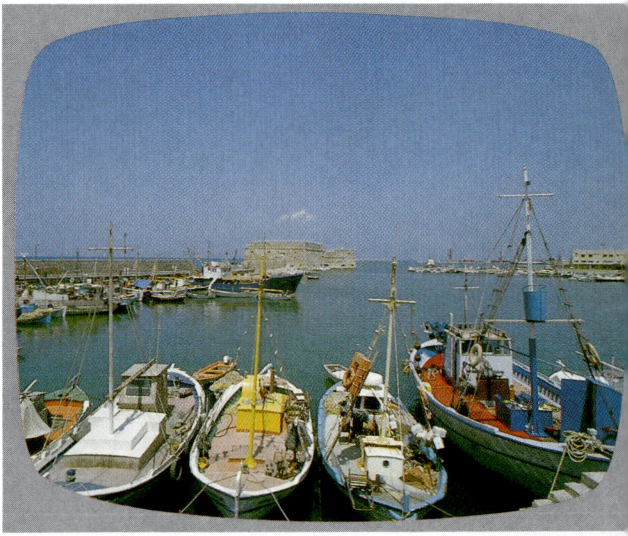

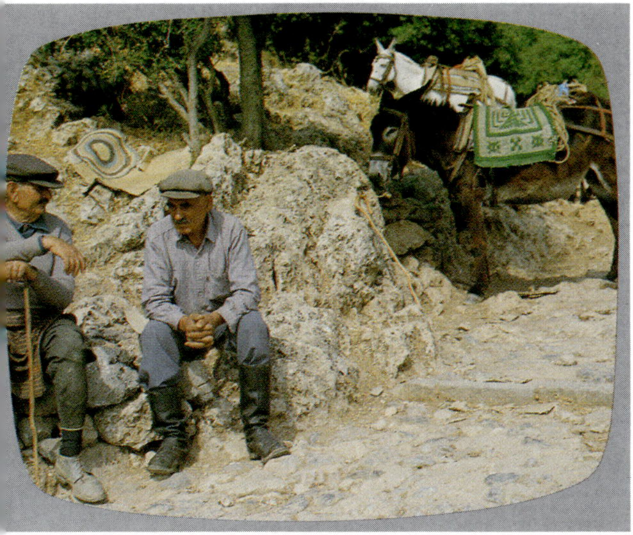

You will only captivate your audience with scenes which tell a story about the place and the people you spent your holiday with. Whether it's the Greeks with their donkeys...

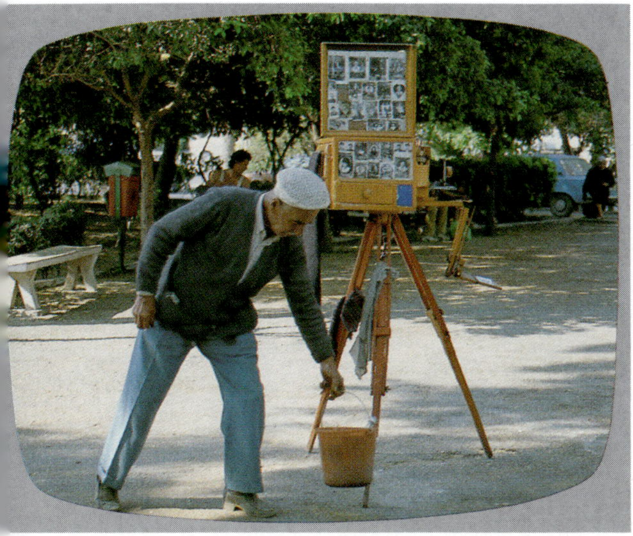

...or the photographer waiting for customers. The images describe life on the island. Language, music and sounds can complement and intensify the visual impression.

Children, children: The dear little ones - you can't watch them too often with the camcorder. They forget you are there...

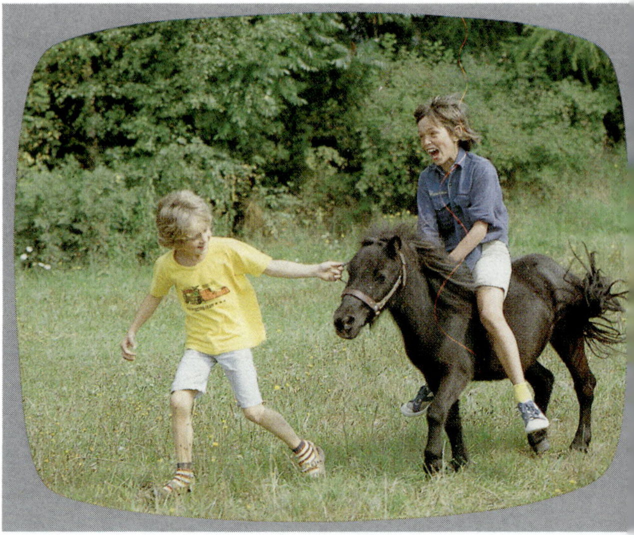

...while concentrating on staying aboard and keeping out the way of flying hooves!

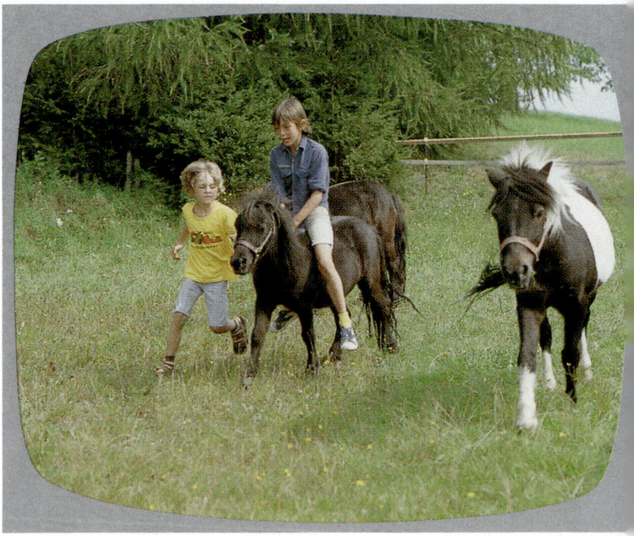

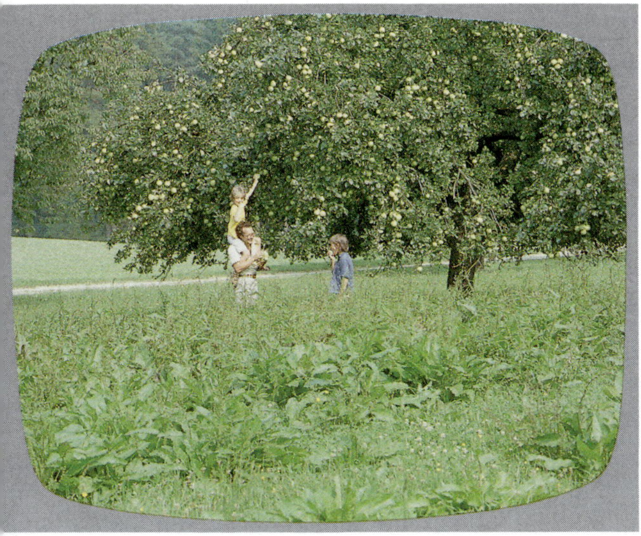

Children like playing the leading parts, as long as you don't make them repeat scenes too many times. But...

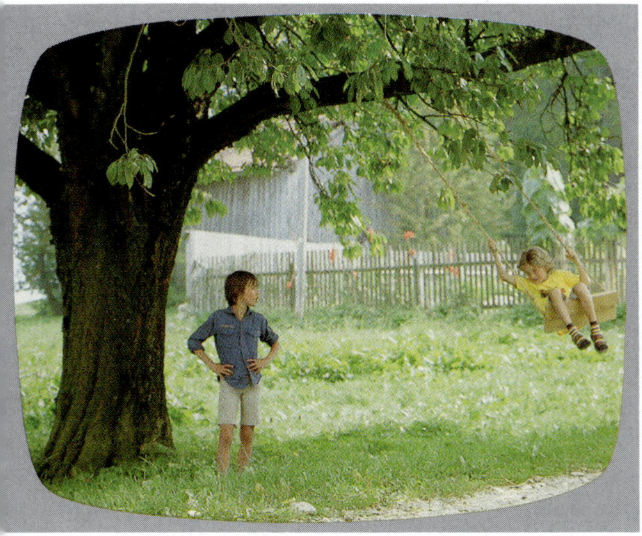

...it mustn't be boring. When picking apples or playing on the swings they will have plenty of fun. And children will enjoy the video film just as much as you do.

Historic festivals: where can you get the actors for your costume drama for nothing? At historic festivals organised...

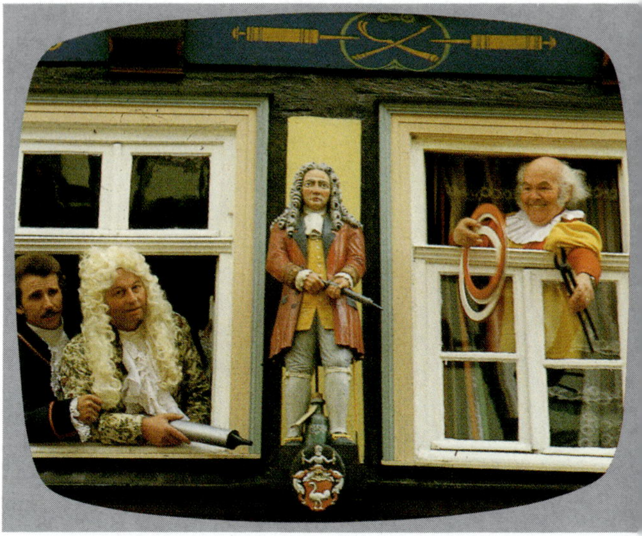

...by towns and communities, like this Dr. Iron Beard show in Germany. It is very important to select the best vantage points for your shots in advance, if that's possible.

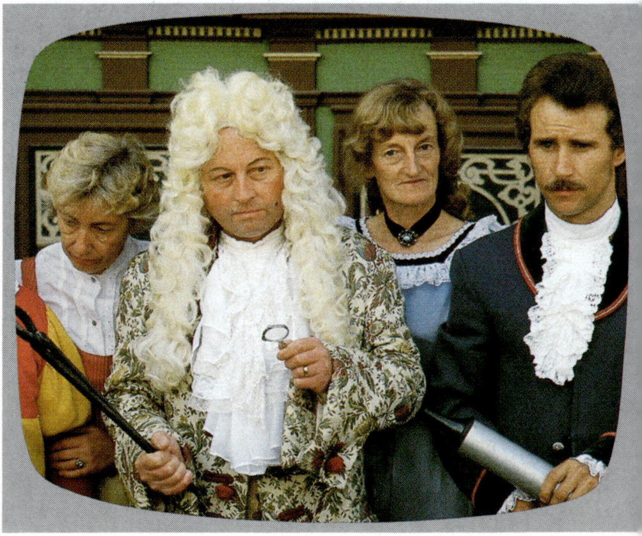

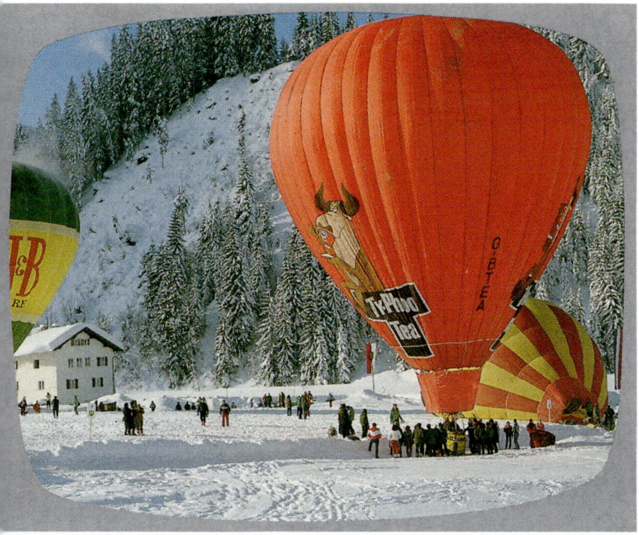

Enjoying sports: Sun, snow, a bright blue sky and a hot air balloon rally. It makes the video film-maker's heart sing: whether it's take-off...

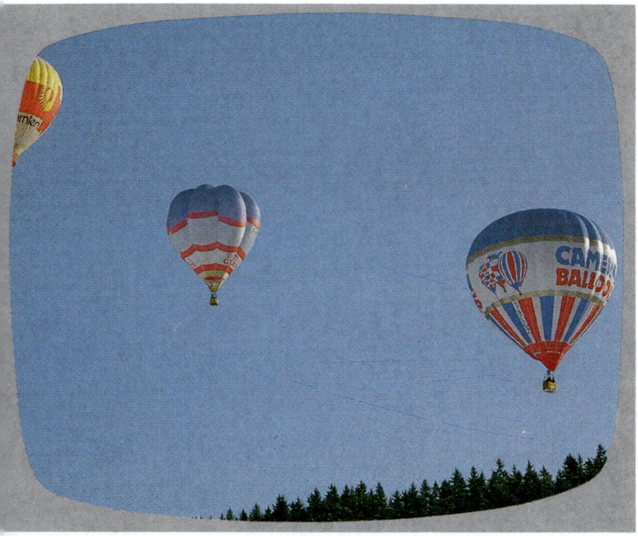

...or mid-flight shots - the subjects are endless. Often you can ride along as a guest and record events from a bird's eye view.

Animals are great: baby elephants are as playful as small children. A reason for every video film-maker to reach for the camcorder...

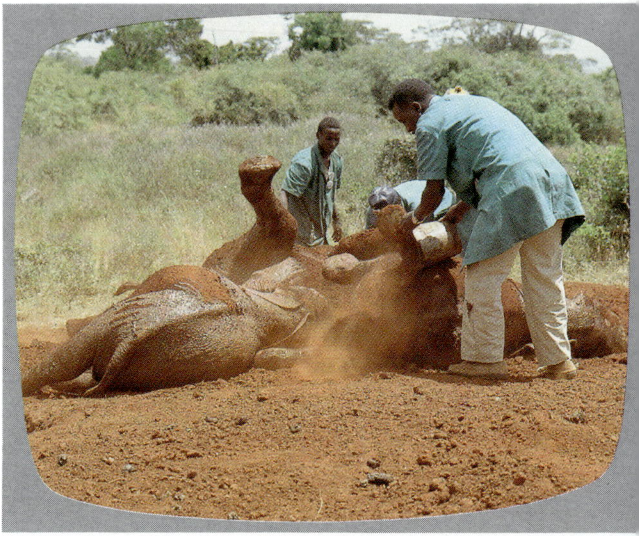

...and have a go at filming animals. With a little patience and stamina you will get superb videos.

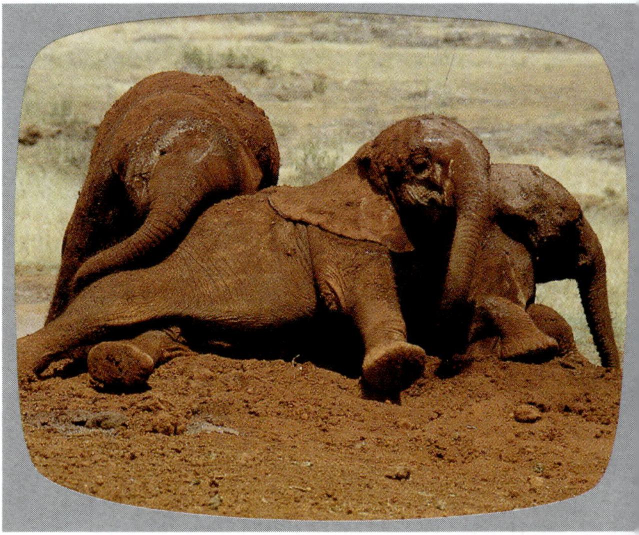

Expensive décor therefore signals prosperity, as do choice jewelry, a luxury car and so on. Any other lifestyle can be signalled in a similar way with the appropriate choice of a few props

But props can also take on central parts: just think of stories about the hunt for a hidden treasure, or a key holding a secret, a car undertaking a trip, or a ring lost at the scene of a murder.

These offer fantastic opportunities of moving on a story or creating suspense, without the need for particularly sophisticated techniques. Props as the stars of a film: discover this simple method of having a thread run through the story in a captivating manner!

Lighting

Most film-makers believe that you need lights only when it is getting dark and the speed of the camcorder is no longer sufficient. Completely wrong! Filming with lights in the light is one of the most elementary principles of filming; light effects can conjure up unique and characteristic moods, which clarify, or cleverly emphasise, the message of the participants and locations. Light and shadow are inextricably linked: used purposefully, they contribute substantially to the job of image composition. This wisdom should shine brightly in the heads of film-makers! Different types of light need to be distinguished for filming:

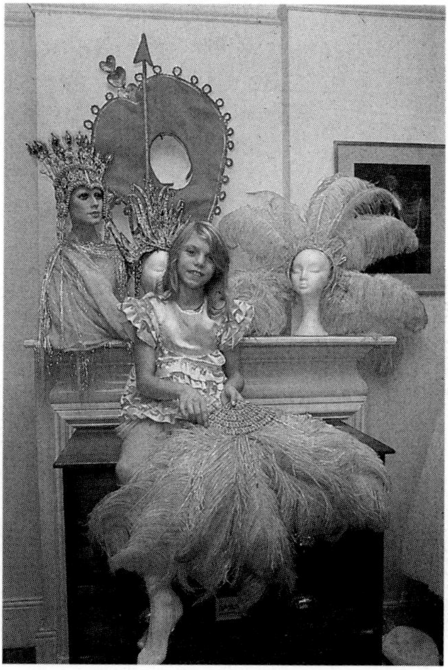

Good sets and costumes make more of every film and contribute more to a better understanding of the action.

- The main light with the highest illumination intensity imitates the natural source of light.
- Fill-in light has the task of lighting up the shadows created by the main light.
- Frontal light falls onto the subject to be filmed along the optical axis of the camera and moves it into the centre.

● Key light is a special light source which creates an attractive shiny effect in the eyes of an actor.

● Side light gives an additional three-dimensional quality to the image by tracing the contours and structures of subjects. Moreover, you can achieve pretty fill-in and optically flattering effects with silver and gold foil panels.

Make-up

Nothing makes a film more interesting than good make-up. Despite the best acting abilities, a film can win or lose because of the work of the make-up artists. Three-day beards, artificially bald heads, gaping wounds - we all know the repertoire of the illusion surgeons, who literally conjure up works of art. But you don't always need bits of flapping skin to contribute to the success of a film; a film will also benefit from the art of make-up: you can imitate old skin with latex; skin glow gel is suitable for showing wet or sweaty skin; a tear stick produces natural tears; and even a lay person should manage to sculpt a distinctive nose out of plasticine.

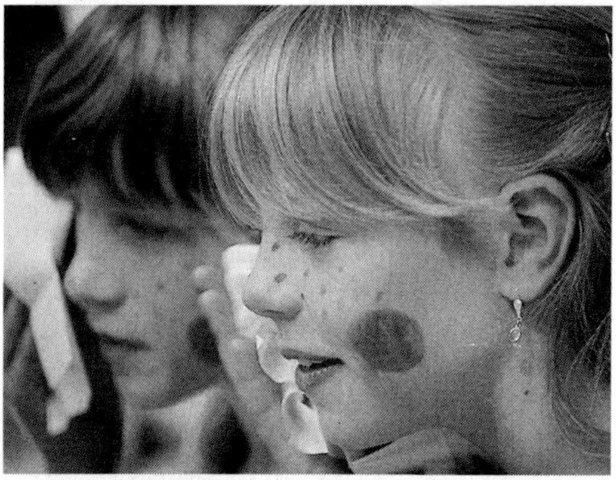

Make-up doesn't have to be sophisticated. Small tricks often have great effects.

The Production

Continuity

No film has ever been filmed from beginning to end in the actual order of events. The reasons for this are as follows:

1. You might have to keep driving backwards and forwards between the different locations.

2. You proceed economically, for example shooting all interior scenes when the weather is bad.

3. Scenes usually turn out too long and have to be shortened by editing.

This means that parts of the film will need to be joined together. The joining combines the images and determines a certain tempo with the rhythm of editing sequences. It is important in editing that each frame follows on logically from the previous one. Continuity mistakes are often noticeable even in cinema films, for example when a conversation is shot by cutting between the characters and one actor's cigarette has suddenly burned down after one cut, even though only seconds have passed; or if an actor suddenly has designer stubble because a scene took too long to work on and the normal beard growth has taken its toll. It's better to watch out for this sort of thing than put up with expensive re-shooting.

Transitions

A group of monkeys in the desert is fighting over a water hole. One of them suddenly discovers the power of a bone that is lying about and batters its opponent over the head. It then throws the bone into the air with a triumphant shout. As the bone spirals away into the distance it turns into a space station.

This scene is from the film *2001 - A Space Odyssey*, and it is a masterpiece by its director Stanley Kubrick who used this ingenious transition to bridge millions of years between the Stone Age and the future.

But you don't have to come up with a stroke of genius to enrich your film with sophisticated transitions: simple out-of-focus transitions, where one scene ends as a blurred image and the next one also begins blurred, are enormously effective. Or a hi-speed pan, where the camera is rapidly moved in the horizontal whilst a scene ends and a new one begins. Or a symbolic cut, for example a shoot-out starting at the precise moment when the camera focuses on a bowling ball hitting all nine pins during a bowling match taking place in the same room. Or the simplest method: fading. There are plenty of examples, and even more ideas if you want them.

The Axis Jump

The axis jump isn't an Olympic discipline but an imaginary action line, for example between two characters, which must not be crossed in front of the camera during recording. If this does happen, it is called an axis jump which can confuse the audience by reversing the positions of the characters (left becomes right, and vice versa).

Such a mistake can happen in the excitement of filming. It can only be corrected by an intermediate cut which prepares for such a change of positions. This could be an overview shot of the scene to help the audience find their bearings; or it could be a shot of a neutral person watching the scene and whose perspective the camera assumes subsequently.

The Zoom

One masterpiece of optical art unfortunately presents a great temptation: the vario lens - or zoom - and its indiscriminate use. You often see films which contain enough zoom work to give the impression that they were trying to emulate pop music videos. The zoom does allow you to select any image section you like, but this is easily overdone. Bringing a subject close and pushing it away becomes the favourite pastime of many film-makers, but it is often done without any logical reason in terms of the action, and usually at unsuitable speeds.

It is often overlooked that a real (but more complicated) dolly shot, where the camera moves towards the subject, creates a much better spatial impression, resulting in an exciting view of perspective at both sides. This effect is intensified by turning the camera to the right or left to discover new angles of view. As so often, 'less is more' in zooming, too.

Panning

Film is life, and that means movement. The same goes for the camera, which can be tilted along its horizontal and vertical axes and can therefore give the audience an overview, guide their eyes, follow moving subjects or simply have a rhythmic effect. Like all camera movements, panning should always be motivated by the content of the image. Depending on the mood and content of the film scene,

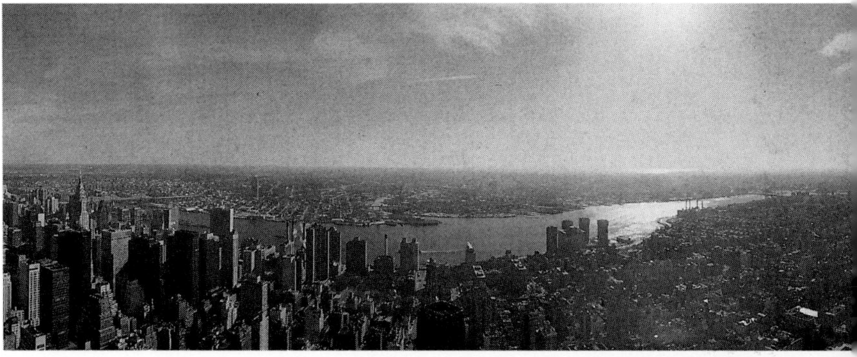

a pan can be slow or fast, even to an abrupt movement from one subject to another - the wrench pan. Experts use a tripod for this, of course, otherwise the shots will look as though they had been taken during a force eight gale...

Camera panning gives the audience an impression of the location, as here of New York's skyline.

Camera Dollying

Camera dollying is used when the audience is to be guided, or when a character is to be followed.

Mounted on a moveable tripod, the camera can deliver constantly changing perspectives. New, previously concealed things become visible, and the viewers feel as if they were moving across the room themselves.

The highlight of camera dollying is the so-called unchained camera, when it is taken off the tripod and becomes a participant itself, for example when it tracks, and moves within, a group of dancers. This puts life into the shot.

The Overall Shot

Every film image shown is an excerpt from reality, selected and determined by the camera, or rather the cameraman. Depending on whether an image section shows more or less reality, you select a setting size whose largest possible frame forms the overall view. This enables you to show the audience the place of the action, to make orientation easier for them, and to introduce them to events. It is useful at the beginning of a film, where it introduces landscapes or city scenes, usually with atmospheric music. It is important to linger on these shots; they contain a wealth of information which needs to be recognized and registered by the audience.

A wider angle is particularly suitable for group shots.

The Two-thirds Shot

The two-thirds shot guides the viewer closer to the subject, enables initial characterisation and slightly reduces the field of vision of the overall shot. It is more suitable for video films than a overall shot because the resolution of the video image is limited and suppresses details.

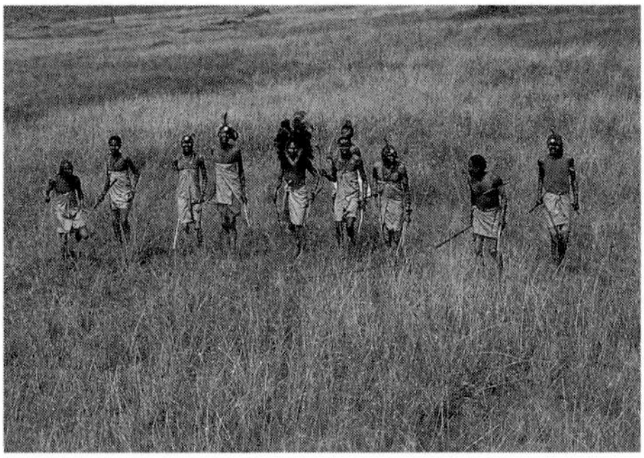

The two-thirds shot is therefore adequate for video: people have elbow room, and respective locations and the scene of action can be recognized.

It also borders on a very popular setting size, the so-called American one from Westerns. It describes the section between the actor's head and his Colt 45.

The Close-up Shot

The close-up shot very deliberately guides the audience's attention to the facial expressions of the actors. The head fills the frame, and the audience can't look past it.

It offers the most expressive form. Used sparingly and purposefully it emphasises highlights in the action. Relentless as a dissecting knife, it exposes intimate emotions, eliminates everything that is contrived and puts the subject in the centre. But watch out: it is also a joker which, when played at the right time, shows whether the player, or rather the cameraman, knows his stuff.

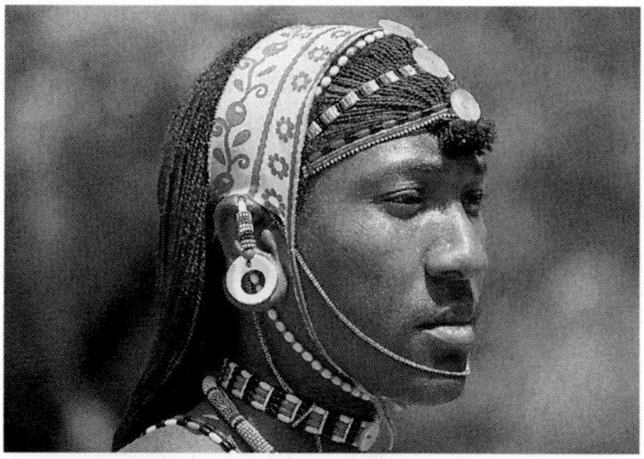

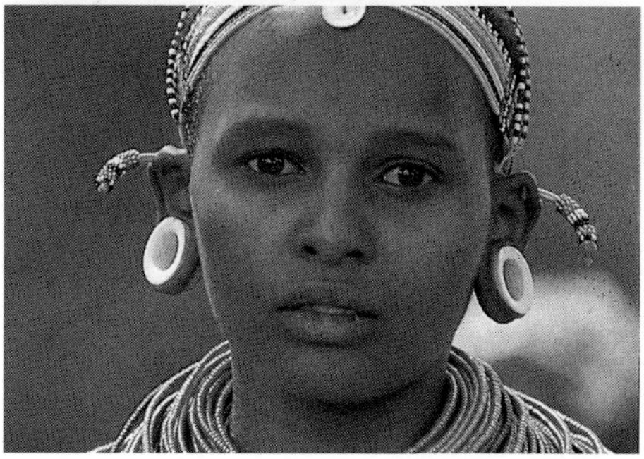

The close-up shot moves the subject into the foreground and captivates the audience.

Exterior Shots

The whole world lies at the video film-maker's feet if he leaves his own four walls in order to capture documentary or staged scenes, work or play, nature or technology. But you should still watch out for a few things in order to avoid any nasty surprises.

This starts with the spare battery pack if you want to prevent your viewfinder from blacking-out when you're in the middle of the most beautiful prairie, and it ends with a spare empty tape.

You should also get information in advance so that you don't end up standing in the airport not knowing whether cameras are allowed into your host country, or even whether airport security regulations let you through the gate with your equipment. These days, this is very important.

Of course, you also have to consider the voltage of other countries if you want to recharge your battery pack. Last, but not least, a little sticky tape, a screwdriver and a piece of florist's wire can help you tackle minor technical problems, for example when something is stuck or wobbly. A colour control monitor can protect you against unwelcome surprises in case the camcorder makes things look rather too colourful to be true.

Interior Shots

You can go about interior shots with far more peace of mind, for at least you've got everything to hand. You'll easily find sockets for the necessary lights, the floor can be perfectly prepared for dollying, and the sound engineer won't have any nasty surprises from low-flying aircraft or police sirens which are always a threat outside.

However, your fuse box should be able to cope with the high power consumption of multiple lights; you should unplug the telephone before you start filming; and your spouse or partner should at least be prepared to grin and bear it. Otherwise the whole thing could turn into a real life drama - although even those have been known to become cinema successes...

Additional lighting is almost indispensable for interior video filming. Light adds colour and sharpness to the image.

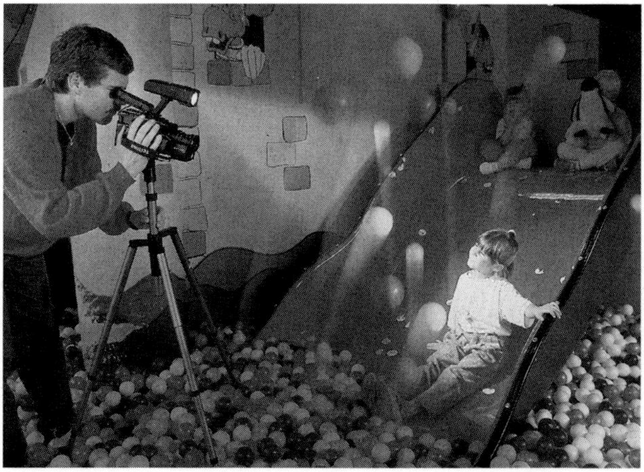

Light and Contrast

Natural light and normal room lighting are often not enough to guarantee good video recordings. You can rarely get by without additional lights. Where there is a lot of light, there is also a lot of shade. Shadows are areas of low light intensity in a scene lit at higher intensity. The brighter the light, the higher the contrast with the shadows. Unfortunately the high expectations many videographers have in terms of lens speed are the result of an over-emphasis on technical data.

Lux is the scientific term for light intensity. It can be defined in the following way: the illumination on the surface of a sphere of one metre radius from a uniform light source of 1 candela placed at its centre is 1 Lux. All camcorder manufacturers advertise extremely low minimum light requirements of between approximately 6 and 10 Lux, giving the impression that you can film by candlelight. In principle you can film by candlelight. The flame of the candle will come out best. Everything else is pitch black, or electronically amplified grainy snow. This becomes particularly obvious if you try lighting a candle in a dark room while the video camera is running, perhaps already directly connected to the TV set. Then compare the monitor image and the result on the TV screen. Only when you switch on a light bulb as well will the room slowly appear, and you will be able to see contours. Even if you can already see surprisingly many nuances of grey on the camcorder monitor, the colour reproduction still looks as if the recording were covered by a grey veil. As the lens has to be fully opened, the depth of field is also very shallow. Smear effects, too, appear surprisingly quickly in low amounts of light. Colours are recognisable from a basic light intensity of 300 Lux. But a clean, brilliant video image appears only when there is sufficient light, at about 800 Lux.

"A point light source of 1 candela at the centre of a sphere of radius one metre produces one Lux on the surface of the sphere."

The first rule of videography must be: There is colour only where there is light. But the colours are right only if you don't mix light sources with different colour temperatures. A scene at a window, lit by daylight flooding in from outside, can't be lit by a video light without causing a colour cast. Even the most perfect white balance will fail here. However, the problems of mixing daylight and artificial light are solved relatively quickly once the videographer knows the differences between colour temperatures, and uses light not only as brightness but also to create moods and colours. More on this later.

Lighting Interior Shots

With interior shots the image quality depends largely on the lighting, and sometimes on the number of lights. The camcorder can light correctly in a surprisingly wide brightness range, but it can't decide whether the correct, optimum lighting was used. This means that the subject needs to be lit correctly in dramatic terms, and that the overall scene should be lit relatively evenly. Even lighting is far more important in video films than is generally believed. Unlike photographic film, the electronics of the camcorder can't cope with a contrast range above 1:16. This means that, when you are aiming for maximum technical quality, the difference in brightness between the darkest and lightest part of a video image must only cover a maximum difference of four aperture stops. This difference is easily and precisely established by metering using the telephoto setting of the zoom lens, the brightest subject details - the lights - and the darkest, the parts in the shade. Regular metering is particularly advisable if you are a beginner or have little experience. In this way you can develop a much better feeling for subject contrast and also for technically-correct lighting.

Before your start lighting, take time and have a good read of the instruction manual that comes with your video light and make sure that everything is suitable for home use. This is not important when using video lights on camera because portable units carry their own power, but when you start to plug into electrical power circuits, please be sure to follow the manufacturers' written recommendations.

Lighting is very important in the continued quality of your video films. If you have already filmed some tape outdoors and you want

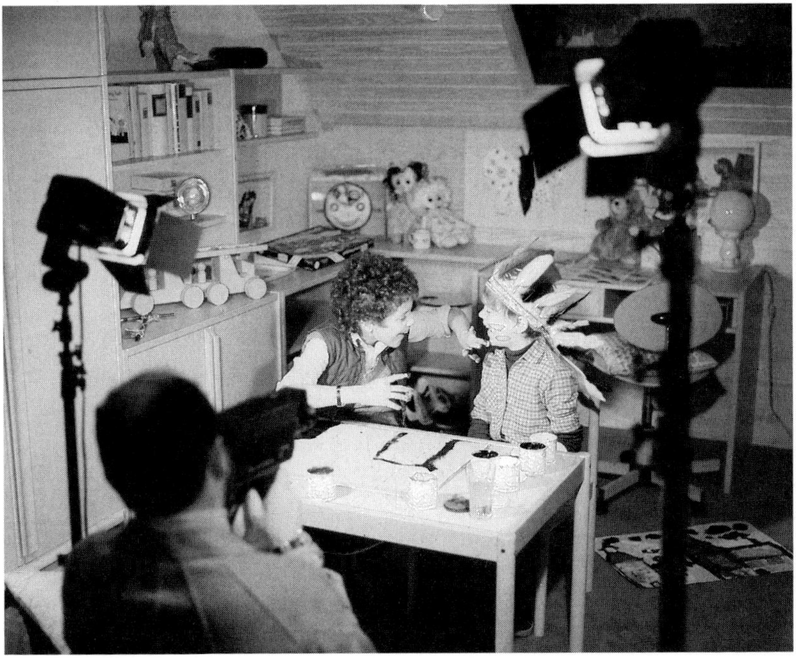

to make sure that you maintain the picture quality and sharpness of daylight video, don't try to film with normal household lighting. It's simply not good enough. The investment in a well-powered but portable video light is well worth the money and will show in the final result of your film. Yes, your camera may work well in low light, but low light shots are more for special effects. For vibrant colour and sharpness, it's important to have proper lighting. The best indoor light of all is bounced light, off a nice white ceiling. This gives a soft overall lighting effect that is very pleasing to both the subject being filmed as well as the end result in your video film.

You can decide between four technical methods of lighting:

Light adds colour to the image. Although modern camcorders can work with small amounts of light, the image quality is noticeably improved when video lights are used.

1. The video light, equipped with a low voltage quartz lamp and powered from the mains or by a NiCad battery.

2. A powerful glow lamp or a special photographic light, often known as a nitraphot lamp, which is used in a clip-on light.

3. The halogen light, delivering between 500 and 2000 watts of light. It is available with or without a ventilator and supplies enough light for a whole room.

4. A studio light, which emits quartz halogen light, delivers approximately 1000 watts of light. It has the effect of a relatively diffuse floodlight.

The following sections describe the advantages and disadvantages of different light sources, as well as their respective technical and creative applications in videography.

The Video Light

The video light is certainly the most popular light source of all. It helps in many varied situations, even when run from a battery pack for exterior shots. In general use, it is the ideal added light source. Some low-powered lights may not be enough for full interior shots, but they usually fit in well with the other lighting. Moving subjects in particular profit from this additional light, especially if the basic light is not very bright. As a fill-in light by itself the video light is used for backlit shots at the window, for example, or as support in candle-lit situations.

The above-mentioned rule about four aperture stops difference in brightness for maximum technical quality applies also, of course, to exterior shots. This is why you should always take along the video light if it is powered by a battery pack. Despite its artificial character, its concentrated and relatively hard light can be used to improve colours on all subjects which are not too large. In portrait shots in particular it improves the reproduction of skin tones, which appear warmer.

The video light market, especially for quality battery-powered lights, has seen massive acceptance in recent years, ranging from 6 volt/15-watt to 300-watt lights. Powerful video lights sometimes have a fan, whose ventilator sounds are readily picked up by the microphone. But there are already 300 watt video lights which work without a ventilator, and are therefore silent.

The multitude of features shows clearly the importance of battery-powered lights for industry and film-makers. The reflectors were first to be improved. Optimized, computer-designed reflectors provide a surprisingly even spread of light, for the wide-angle range as well as telephoto settings. The dreaded hot spot, where the centre of the image gets full light and the light reduces in a circular pattern towards the edge, is now only to be found on the cheapest and most basic lights which are not recommended. Many video lights can be tilted to facilitate indirect lighting, ideal for close-up shots or scenes happening a metre or two from the camera. But even then it is not always necessary, at least not for lighting reasons; the top video lights have an integral electronic system and a sensor which calculate the amount of light required and control the brightness of the lamp. Every subject filmed with an additional light is therefore reproduced with a greater wealth of details and more colour intensity.

The trend in video lights is clearly towards the light being on the accessory shoe, with its own battery power. Increasing emphasis is also being placed on universal current supply, so there are already a variety of battery packs, lead or NiCad, mains adaptors and car battery attachments for a multitude of lights. It should also be noted that some camcorder and light battery packs are already interchangeable.

This is a considerable convenience, particularly if you get into situations where you don't have access to a power socket for hours or days, as for example on a sailing trip. The capacity of a battery-powered video light is between 10 and 50 minutes, depending on the power supply. Any flaps, whether they come with the light or are available as accessories, are not meant for controlling the brightness, but to help guide the light precisely. Experts call these metal flaps Barn Doors, but they are more important on the spots and other lights

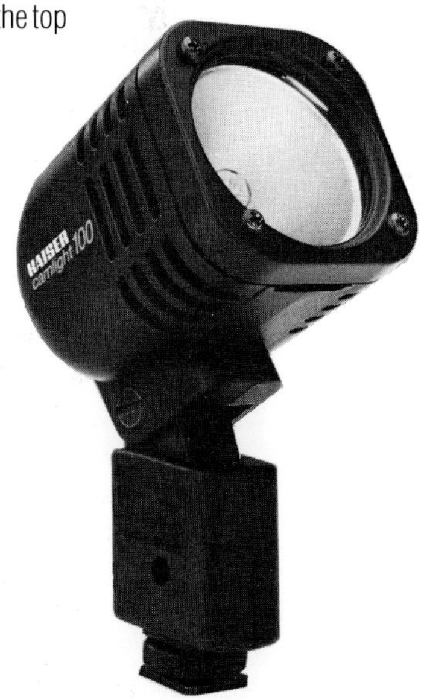

Portable video lights are pushed onto the accessory shoe of the camcorder.

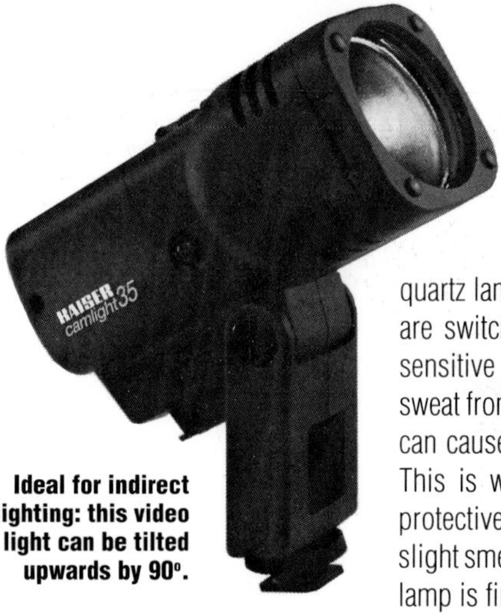

Ideal for indirect lighting: this video light can be tilted upwards by 90°.

described below than on battery-powered lights. For security reasons there should always be a safety glass or other shatter protection in front of the battery-powered light. This is because quartz lamps can burn out and explode when they are switched on. All quartz lamps are extremely sensitive to soiling on the glass envelope. Even sweat from your fingers touching the glass directly can cause the light to burn out relatively quickly. This is why replacement lamps are supplied in protective packing, only removed after insertion. A slight smell or noticeable steaming when the quartz lamp is first switched on is not unusual.

Basic Lighting

The main requirement with interior shots is to increase the general brightness of the room to the necessary intensity in all those areas where film events take place. This demands a higher degree of lighting and cannot always be achieved with clip-on video lights. The rule that light intensity decreases by a factor equal to the square of the distance from the source - the inverse square law - applies to all lights. This means that the intensity of a beam of light emitted by a point-shaped light source is reduced by a factor which is the square of the distance from it. If the intensity of a light source determined for this beam of light has a value of 1 at a certain distance, it will only have the value of 1 : (2 x 2) = $^1/4$ at twice that distance, and only 1 : (3 x 3) = $^1/9$ at three times the distance. A small low voltage or halogen lamp may be considered a point light source.

This is the usual reason why the background - particularly on interior shots - often gives the impression of night recordings, something that can be improved with added light.

A special photographic light, also known as a nitraphot lamp, is more than a stopgap against excessively dark backgrounds. Such filament lamps have reflective interior surfaces and matt sides, which emit the correct colour temperature by means of a special

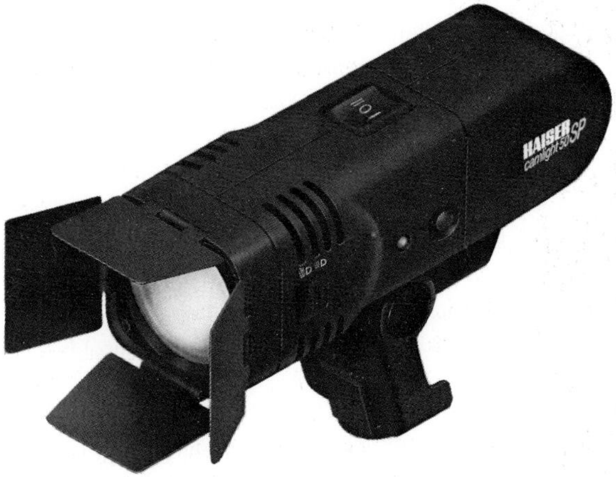

Some video lights are fitted with four barn doors to allow precise light positioning.

coating. These lamps are available as (blue) daylight or artificial light types. With a light performance of 60 or 100 watts they are well-suited for lighting titles, repro or close-up shots. With 150 or 250 watts they are sufficient for filling in, or suitable as highlighters. With a performance of 500 watts they can provide a cheap and interesting alternative for lighting interiors. Reflector lamps of 500 watts should not be lit for more than five minutes at a time because they develop a large amount of heat. They are easily used in conjunction with clip-on lights, which consist only of a lamp holder and a sturdy clip. Superior versions have an additional joint which increases the possibilities of mobility and adjustment. Space permitting, these lamps should be set up behind, or to the side of, the photographer, but in any case concealed. Their light should be aimed at a (white or colourless) side wall, ceiling or panel.

The inverse square law no longer applies because the light, with the light reflected from the ceiling, is no longer a point-shaped light source. The room can be lit evenly - the larger the area lit on the ceiling (or the side), the better. In order to enable the amateur film-maker to influence the size of the area more precisely, some lights are fitted with a tripod thread rather than a clip. The primary advantage is not that the light can be set up on the tripod, but that photo umbrellas are available for use with tripods or lighting stands.

They are particularly good at diffusing transmitted or fully reflecting light. Harsh shadows are less frequent in this way.

Halogen Lamps

These reflecting umbrellas are also to be recommended for halogen lights, which are available up to 2000 watts and have their own reflectors and light tubs in order to produce particularly soft light. In fact, this type of lamp can now be converted into a focusable spot light to achieve exactly the opposite effect, a clearly definable spot. Although the sound of the ventilators has been reduced to a minimum, make sure that there isn't a microphone nearby.

As daylight filters, barn doors and other attachments are available for halogen lamps, they can also be used for special types of lighting. However, their main task is probably the creation of a basic brightness. Direct light - without any adjustment - is rarely advisable because halogen lamps produce relatively hard light which casts harsh shadows behind objects and people. They are therefore more suitable as background and fill-in lights, and are good for indirect lighting via the ceiling because of their light intensity. Children in particular quickly get used to this type of light. But be careful! Light reflecting purely from above intensifies shadows in the eye socket, and the nose can also cast unnatural shadows. This can be avoided with a small battery-powered light on the camera for filling in these impending shadows. You should also beware of over-lighting a room; the heat from several large lamps can quickly spoil the participants' video fun and well and truly destroy the atmosphere. At an anniversary dinner, for example, use a few 250 watt lamps around the table and a battery-powered light on the video camera.

Studio Lights

You will be familiar with extremely bright halogen lamps from many shop windows; these are also available as studio lights. Even if they are offered as daylight or artificial light types you should be careful if they are not purely photographic or video lights. The reason for this is that the colour temperature says nothing about the spectral composition of the light. If this is not even, you can get inexplicable colour casts. Most of these studio lights can easily be diffused as floodlights and therefore ensure a good basic brightness.

The basic brightness is also important for a portrait shot, and additional lights contribute dramatic lighting effects. As a basic rule, fill-in light should have a maximum intensity of half that of the main light. This can be determined with a light meter; it should indicate one aperture stop less for the filled-in shadow section than for the lit subject.

The background light also needs to be mentioned once more. Similar to an effect light, it has the task of separating people and objects from the background. Sufficiently bright background light also ensures that there aren't any big colour jumps within scenes. This is particularly intrusive on changing image sections.

But the light intensity for the background should stay noticeably behind the lighting for the main subject and is particularly effective if it softly lights the background. Sometimes it is enough to build small islands of light into the background, for example by switching on available room lights or fitting them with more powerful bulbs.

Particular manifestations of light, usually created with an additional light, are known as effect lights; these could be light seams, light stains or highlights.

There is also a special type of lighting which has proved useful for reporting and interviews. For example, when two people are to be filmed in an interview, two lights are used. They are set at an angle of 30° to the subject and shine down from above. They provide frontal light for one person, back lighting for the other, and vice versa.

The Kaiser Studiolight 2000 with a lighting performance of 2000 watts, four barn door attachment, filter compartments and safety fan allows professional studio lighting.

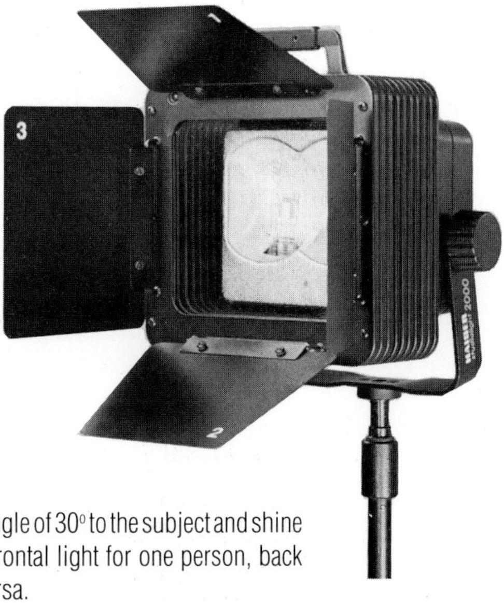

At the very beginning of this chapter we pointed out that you can't really film anything other than the candle's flame in candle light. But with correct lighting even this becomes possible: by using the sparse light of a video light, possibly diffused and with the diffusion zone limited by barn doors, for it must not cast a shadow of its own and is only supposed to improve the light of the candle. If the candle is in a candlestick on the table, the light cast by the battery-powered light can come from the ceiling for intensification, just filling in the shadows of the candle light and the scene around it.

The Battery Pack

You can't film without power: this is provided by the battery pack. It is the only real trouble-maker in video filming. It is guaranteed always to tell you that it can no longer provide enough power at just the wrong time. Its capacity depends on its chemical composition and size: a mini-battery pack has a capacity of 1000 milliamperes per hour (mAh), and the largest capacity is currently about 2400 mAh. If this isn't enough for you, you have to budget for spare battery packs or even invest in a battery belt. But in order to get top performance from one or more battery packs, you should follow a few basic rules.

Beginners in particular use far more power than is necessary or desirable, for example by not switching off the camcorder. In every pause between recordings, the head drum rotates, the viewfinder monitor produces an image, and the autofocus motor adjusts the focusing elements as soon as something moves in front of the camera. Even frequent zooming in and out with the zoom lens, and playing back the recorded scenes, cause increased power consumption. In addition, there is the unpleasant characteristic of all battery packs that they continuously discharge themselves. The battery pack delivers the highest yield of energy at an ambient temperature of approximately 20°C. At minus 20°C its performance is reduced by half. And if the pack isn't used for several months it can discharge itself to such a degree that proper charging is no longer possible. If one of the single batteries (camcorder battery packs usually consist of several batteries) has gone into a deep state of

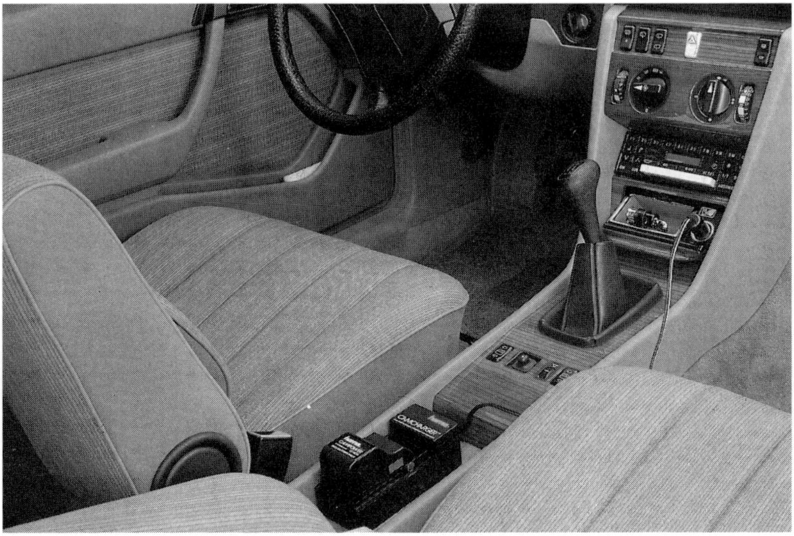

The cigarette lighter of a car is a most convenient place for charging camcorder battery packs.

discharge, charging will no longer be possible at all. A battery pack can normally be recharged more than a thousand times, and therefore deserves some attention. A brand new battery pack will only reach its highest possible storage capacity after several (correct) charging cycles.

Because of this, it should first of all be charged and then discharged, if possible in the camcorder. The battery pack delivers top performance if this procedure is carried out two or three times in a row. If the pack isn't used for a several months, the chemical processes inside the pack slow down, and the procedure should, if possible, be repeated. But don't start by recharging, discharge the pack first! The pack also has a sort of chemical memory, which is often described as a memory effect. If, for example, you recharge a pack even though it hasn't run down, it will remember this and will in future only deliver part of the stored power, telling you it is empty far too early. This is why a battery pack should be discharged by working before it is re-connected to the mains. This applies to all rechargeable batteries, no matter for what purpose they are used.

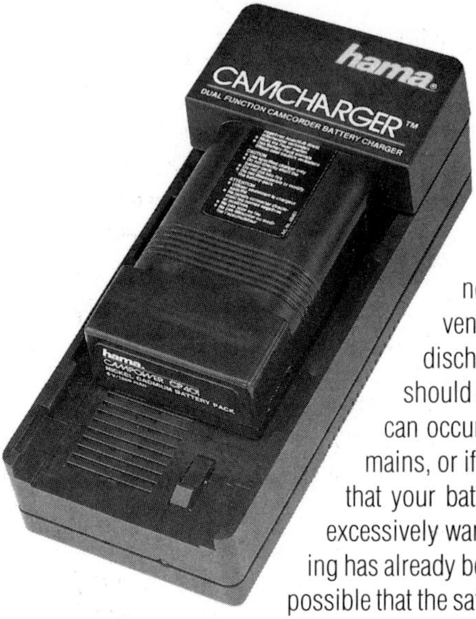

The accessories industry is, of course, aware of the consumers' negligence in handling battery packs, and many companies have developed mains and charging devices which check and discharge the pack by means of sophisticated switching circuits before fully recharging. But if you're not sure whether your charger has this convenient feature, you should only ever connect discharged battery packs to the mains, and you should also beware of overcharging. Overcharging can occur if an almost full pack is connected to the mains, or if it is charged for too long. You can assume that your battery pack has been overcharged if it gets excessively warm during the charging process. Discharging has already begun to take place inside the pack. It is also possible that the safety valve has responded by draining off the excess pressure that has arisen. The operating manual of your charger will tell you whether there is a danger of overcharging. Otherwise an overcharged pack, like a completely discharged one, can no longer be used and should be disposed of as special waste in an environmentally friendly way.

Many charging units get their energy for charging camcorder and video light battery packs either from a mains socket or from the cigarette lighter in the car.

Light and Colour Temperature

Colour temperature is measured in kelvins. They indicate the energy distribution of a light source, the spectral composition of the light used for filming. The kelvin scale starts at an absolute zero point of minus 273°. Its gradation corresponds to the Celsius scale. With glowing objects there is a correlation between temperature and colour. For example, red-hot iron has a temperature of approximately 800° Celsius and a colour temperature of approximately 527 kelvins; yellow-glowing iron has a temperature of about 1000° Celsius (727 kelvins); at its melting point at approximately 1500° Celsius iron is white-hot and has a colour temperature of about 1300 kelvins. As the temperature increases, the blue proportion of the light increases, and vice versa: as the colour temperatures decreases, the red proportion increases. These changes in colour appear as colour casts if the recording light has a different colour temperature; that is, if it requires different kelvin values than the basic setting of the white balance. The image will therefore show too high a red proportion (an orange cast) if the recording light has a lower kelvin value than daylight, and a blue cast appears when the kelvin value is higher! The lower the colour temperature, the higher the red proportion. The blue proportion increases with increasing kelvin values.

The table below shows how much the colour temperature can vary. In a daylight setting (standard), everything over 5500 kelvins produces a blue cast, everything under 5500 an orange cast. In artificial light, depending on the basic programming, a daylight situation yields a blue cast, and anything below the value set, an orange cast.

Colour temperature (distribution temperature) of some light sources

Light source	k
Candle light	2000
Bulb (100 watt)	2800
Type B photo lamp (500 watt)	3200
Halogen lamp	3400
Moonlight	4100
Electronic flash	5500
Midday sunlight	6000-8000
Overcast sky	6500-7500
Blue sky	9000-18,000

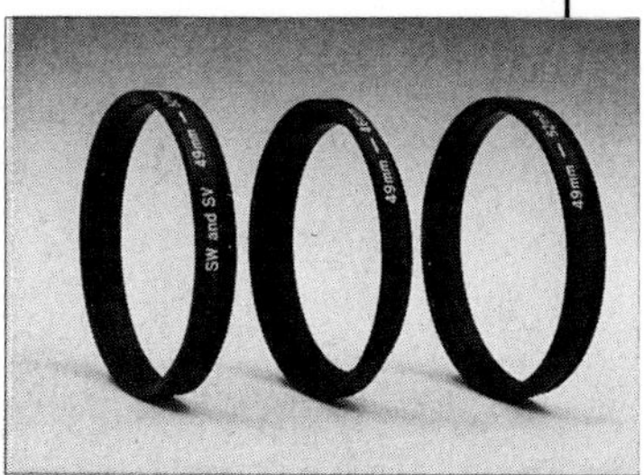

Adaptor rings.

Colour casts can be corrected with the help of the white balance, or by attaching conversion filters. The skylight filter, which is still used all the time by many people, is one such conversion filter: on sunny days (and therefore in higher colour temperatures) its faint pink tint ensures that sections in the shade don't become too blue. In the mountains it is advisable to use the stronger IB instead of the normal skylight filter, or UV filter, which has almost no exposure factor. In the tropics and in the mountains you should use a UV filter - an ultra-violet blocking filter - because the recording chip is sensitive to ultraviolet rays and makes them visible as a blue image. But a UV filter can be left on the lens permanently even though most quality lenses nowadays have their own UV-block layer.

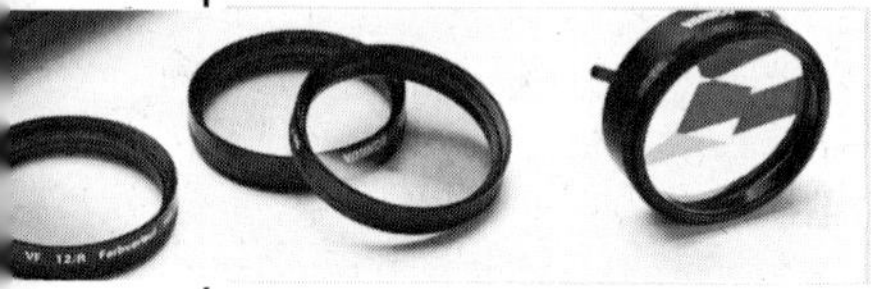

All the filters described are required for a shot where a white object is supposed to stay white, regardless of the lighting by a light source. Whether this is really necessary is up to the videographer. With reproduction or important documentation work you will try to achieve this ideal state. Too much of a good thing (too many filters) can destroy every mood. We even talk about the blue hour, or blue dusk. A colour cast which is necessary for the mood of the subject and should really be made even more obvious for creative reasons, should not be eliminated with filters. You should also remember that corrections are possible at the cutting and editing stage, even if the whole scene has a minimal colour cast.

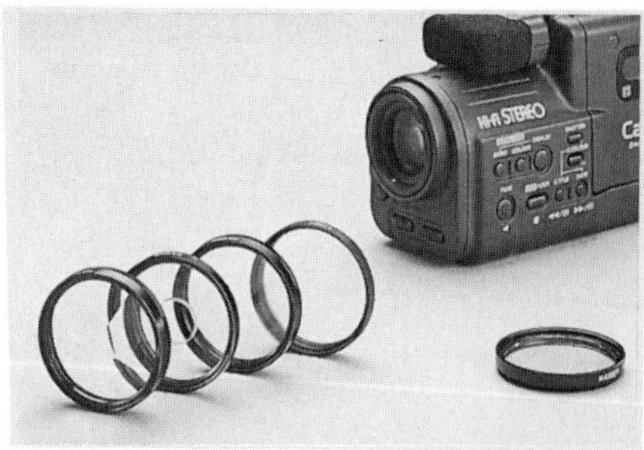

For improved colours: quality filter sets and special effects.

Editing

Admittedly, 95% of video film-makers don't do it - they don't even think about editing their own video films. They watch them straight out of the camcorder, and then put the tape away in a drawer, possibly never to be seen again - and that really is a shame.

Editing can sound rather terrifying - very complicated and highly artistic, and also expensive because of the edit controller. But don't be fooled, this is completely the wrong impression.

Editing means nothing other than copying those parts of the video film you like, or which are somehow important to you, from the original tape (that you filmed onto) to a different cassette.

One frequent argument against editing is that you always lose in quality when copying. This is true. But how much quality you lose depends very much on the quality of the original. Technically good originals will deliver correspondingly good copies.

"Editing means: I copy the parts I like from the original cassette to a different cassette."

This is one important reason why committed video film-makers buy a Video Hi-8 camcorder: resolution (and therefore sharpness and brilliance) and colour purity are much better in Hi-8 than in the standard Video 8 system.

It is also questionable whether your audience will even be concerned by the small loss in quality created by copying.

To start with you won't need more than the following for editing:

- a camcorder;
- a home video recorder, no matter which system.
- a colour TV set, because you want to check on the large monitor which parts you want to copy;
- and two quick thumbs to start and stop the camcorder and video recorder.

If the worst came to the worst you might also need to get hold of some cables or adaptors. But to start with you really don't need anything more for editing.

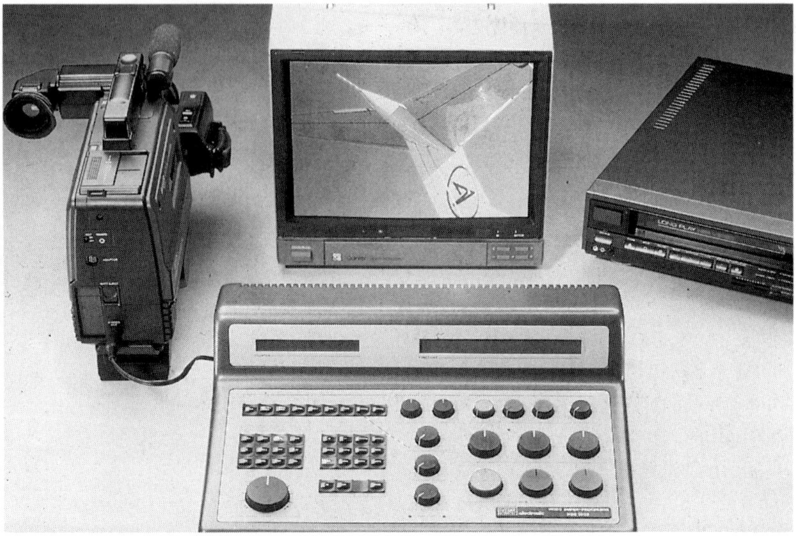

Camcorder, TV set and video recorder are needed for editing. An edit controller makes things even easier.

It is a shame that so few people edit their video recordings. The Video 8 cassette offers a maximum recording length of 90 minutes, which is the most popular length. However, experienced video film-makers prefer the Video 8 cassette with a recording length of 60 or 30 minutes. Video film-makers with Hi-8 camcorders can choose from Hi-8 cassettes (ME tape!) with a recording length of 30, 60 and 90 minutes.

Most of the Video 8 and Video Hi-8 camcorders on offer can also be switched to Long Play mode to double the recording length.

Even the shortest recording length mentioned here is still very long. For the video film-maker it can be an eternity - that is, if you don't just blindly point the camera and shoot. Try to take good shots.

Most beginners will tend to film scenes which are either too long or too short. You should find out which lengths are suitable in which situations.

One Theme - One Cassette!

Only rarely will you find an event that yields enough in visual terms to fill a whole cassette. Even on a video safari in Kenya, where there were plenty of great subjects and we were out and about from sunrise to sunset, we rarely captured more than 30 or 40 minutes worth of good shots.

In terms of everyday video filming this means that we will rarely manage to fill a whole cassette. That is why we end up with very different subjects on one cassette.

If you enjoy video filming you will accumulate four, eight, or even more cassettes over the years. Now imagine Granny has come to visit and you want to show her the shots of her young grandson being cute when he was playing with the little goats in the zoo. How are you going to find those shots from amongst all the others on all those cassettes? You'll end up cursing your fate, and the video performance will become a torture for Granny. There's only one remedy for this kind of disaster: copy all shots of the grandson onto one cassette.

But there's something else: compared to the price of a movie film with sound, video tapes are a bargain; and compared to the three-

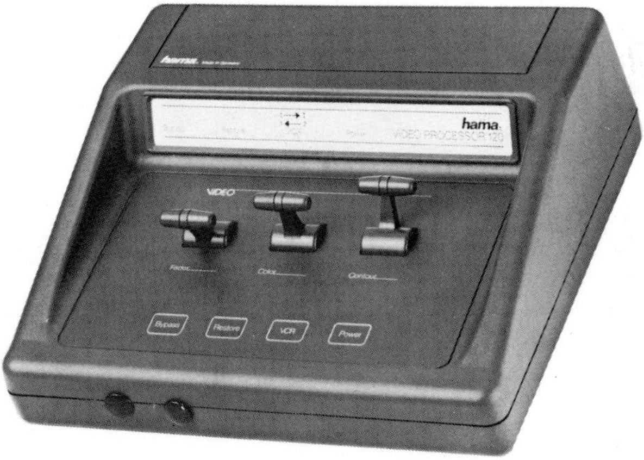

The Hama Video Processor 120 allows, for example, a comparison of corrected and uncorrected scenes.

and-a-half minutes of a movie reel, the cassette offers a massive recording length. This is bad because it tempts you to point and shoot aimlessly with the camcorder, but it is also a blessing because you can afford to keep filming. This is important for several reasons:

- In St Mark's Square in Venice or Trafalgar Square in London, for example, amateur video film-makers often have little or no influence over what happens.
- With children or wild animals you never know what will happen, when and how.

But this means that even the most experienced video film-maker, who never makes mistakes like camera shake, unsharp shots etc, will never manage films without:

- lengths (when nothing happens);
- duds (somebody or something accidentally gets into your shot so you can forget the recording);
- doublettes (you record certain actions several times to make completely sure you get them on tape).

Hours of videos with lengths, duds and doublettes will become a nightmare for your audience; your embarrassed excuses can't improve the disaster; so it's better to edit out all the junk; show your guests ten to fifteen minutes worth of the best, absolute top recordings, and everybody is happy.

How does Editing Work?

You have connected the camcorder, home video recorder and TV set (as the control monitor), switched them on and tuned them (also see the chapter *Plugs, Sockets/Jacks and Adaptors*). If you have done everything correctly you will see the image from the play-back device (the camcorder) on the TV monitor.

It's best to use your camcorder as the play-back device because the technical quality of the reproduction is best on the device used for recording. (The reason: the recording and play-back electronics are tuned perfectly.) You need to switch the camcorder to VCR (see the chapter *Trouble-shooting*). So you're looking for the beginning and end of a good shot on the original cassette. The beginning is called cut-in, the end cut-out. Note the numbers on the counter.

Now load a cassette without record protection into the recording device (your home video recorder); rewind the tape in the camcorder to the cut-in point and switch the recording device to Record/Pause. Then press - simultaneously if possible - the Play button on the camcorder and the Record/Pause button on the home recorder. The edit has started! A glance at the camcorder's counter mechanism will tell you when you are approaching the cut-out point; when you reach it, stop the camcorder play-back and the home video recorder recording - if possible in time, and simultaneously.

You literally need to be quick off the mark, and that's why this method is called the quick thumb method. You then repeat this process with the next good shot, and so on.

However, you need to watch out for one problem, which is to do with the assemble edit ability of your camcorder. Assemble edit means that the camcorder joins one scene to another without producing an image fault at the point where the shots are joined. This sounds easier than it is, so take care.

"The technical quality of the reproduction is best on the device you used for filming"

Your recorder's ability to carry out assemble editing depends a) on when it was made - technology has brought progress - and b) on its sophistication (and therefore also on its price):

- very old and inexpensive video recorders are not usually good;
- old video recorders which aren't very good can only carry out assemble editing if the machine remains in Record/Pause mode. (If you stop the recording altogether, you will later see unpleasant faults at the edit point.)

This is one of the awkward points of the quick thumb method: the home recorder won't stay in Record/Pause mode indefinitely, only for between three and five minutes. After that it automatically switches to Stop.

The reason: in Record/Pause - and Play-back/Pause, ie: Still Image Play-back - mode a lot of strain is put on the magnetic tape - the video heads constantly read the same section of the tape. So if you are working with an older, not very high quality home recorder you need to find the cut-in and cut-out points very quickly so that the separate recordings happen in fast enough succession.

Assemble Editing

Good, relatively recent home video recorders don't have a problem with assemble editing, even if they are switched off completely between two recordings; they automatically search for the last synch pulse on the loaded tape, set themselves in synch with it and join the new recording to the previous one in synch - and you won't see any image faults at the edit point. But you could lose some twenty or more frames at the end of the previous scene, which were simply erased by the video recorder during assemble editing. You therefore have to remember (while you are filming if possible) that every shot should start and end with a sufficiently long still image in order to give you enough meat for editing. Here's an example: fountain/monument/house - a person comes into the frame - looks - walks off again - fountain etc. You can also deliberately work with unsharpness: unsharp - sharp - unsharp. Or with the fade-in and fade-out facility of your camcorder. There are thousands of ways to ensure enough meat for editing. But one thing is 100% certain: if you want to edit shots without still sections at the beginning and end you will have terrible problems - you can really only end up with crash edits.

You also need to think about sound, or more specifically the sound jumps you will get by editing together shots with completely different acoustic moods... For example, a noisy market square - a quiet evening in the park..., so you can begin to see that editing really can be quite an art.

However, this is not to say that hard, or crash edits are completely out of bounds - nothing at all is out of bounds in filming, as long as you do it consciously, deliberately and well.

"If you start and end a scene with a sufficiently long shot, you will have enough meat for editing."

The wise person thinks about editing during filming. But let's get back to the more technical aspects.

As we tried to describe above, quick thumbs aren't the answer to everything. Manufacturers have realised this and have developed devices to aid editing.

One of these is the Edit connection, also called Synchro-Edit. The camcorder and home recorder are connected by means of special built-in sockets/jacks (Control-L or Control-S sockets/jacks) and a control lead cable; a single touch of the Play or Stop button on the camcorder suffices to start or stop the camcorder play-back and home video recorder recording simultaneously.

The Sony SL-V 474 VHS home video recorder is particularly useful for editing. Connected to a monitor, it will show the image of both the play-back device (for example the camcorder) and of the recording device (that is, its own). Secondly, it has the AV-, Control-L and Control-S sockets/jacks at the front (!). Thirdly, its dial allows you to control image play-back forwards and backwards, in Slow and Single frame mode, and therefore enables you to find desired scenes very quickly and really easily.

Integral Editing Devices

Several VHS home recorders have integral editing devices. That's all very well, but it causes a number of problems for Video 8 film-makers.

The Sony SLV-474 VHS home recorder is a great help for editing.

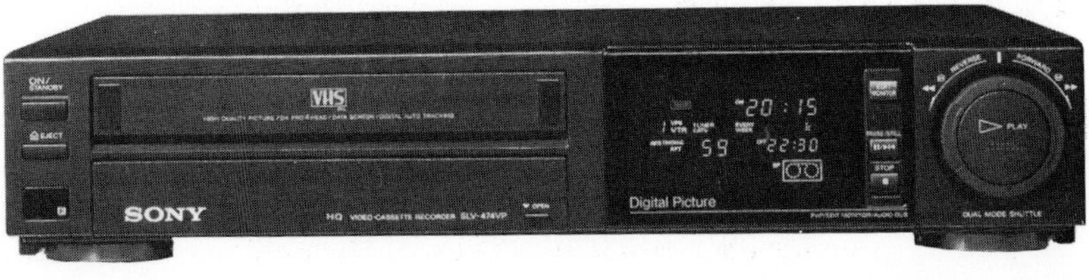

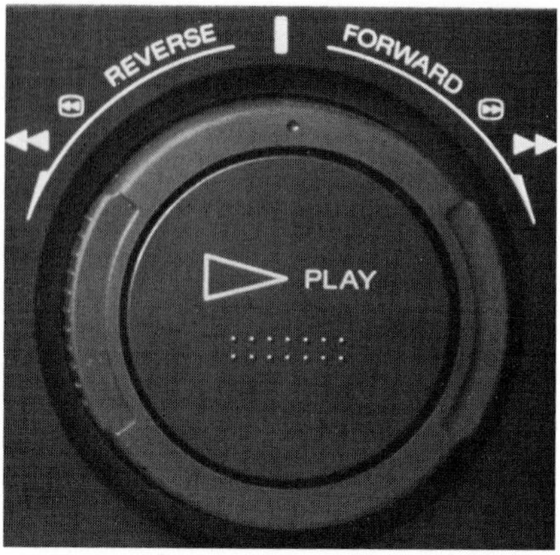

You can precisely control your Sony video recorder with the Dual Mode Shuttle: forward, reverse or slow motion.

Video 8 or Video Hi-8 cassettes can't be played back on a VHS recorder, so they first need to be copied to VHS tapes, which always entails a loss in quality - so we would be editing second generation tape.

If you don't have a second home video recorder the camcorder also has to serve as the recording device, for the final edited copy to be produced in the third (!) generation, that is with a further loss in quality.

But the camcorder can only do this if it has input sockets/jacks for the video (image) and audio (sound) signals. In certain countries, these sockets/jacks increase the price by several per cent because the European Community levies higher import duties on camcorders with input sockets/jacks. This is also why they are not found on every camcorder.

The editing aids and devices mentioned facilitate - without too much effort - the editing of video recordings in the sense of bringing together scenes belonging to one theme. But if you're more ambitious, if you want to add tempo, rhythm and verve to your videos, you will need an edit controller.

A dedicated edit controller searches for the selected cut-in and cut-out points, starting and stopping the play-back and recording accordingly. A dedicated edit controller therefore doesn't influence the video (image) and audio (sound) signals at all - the signal leads run from the play-back device directly into the recording device.

Buying Considerations

You should seek advice from a really experienced salesperson before buying an edit controller. (You'll recognize a really experienced salesperson from the fact that the outlet has edit controllers connected for operation and demonstration, and that the salesperson knows how to operate them.) One of the reasons why detailed advice is required is that the system families Video 8 and VHS need different edit controllers.

In the Video 8 format the counter mechanism of the camcorder sends signals to the Video 8 edit controller. The camcorder counter therefore controls the counter in the edit controller, according to whose data you determine the cut-in and cut-out points. In the VHS family, on the other hand, VITC (Verticle Interval Time Code) - facilitating image-specific editing - became available recently.

"In the Video 8 format the counter mechanism sends signals to the Video 8 edit controller"

An edit controller like this is available for a very modest price. You can determine up to eight cut-in and cut-out points at the touch of a button; you can play these back in the correct order to check them (the Preview facility); you can correct them and then issue the Assemble command at the touch of a button to start the copying process.

Unless you have a photographic memory or take detailed notes, you will only see in Preview mode whether the edits fit together and how, or whether you have made obvious editing mistakes.

Further advantages of an edit controller are: it stores the selected cut-in and cut-out points in case your relatives/friends want them. So you can make as many edited copies as you like from the original tape, and these are, of course, better than copies of the edited tape.

But the edit controller doesn't just store the data you input. It also 'knows' quite a lot more, for example the pre-roll times of your camcorder and home video recorder.

What does that mean? If you press a button on your camcorder or home video recorder, a whole series of actions start up in the machine before it can start the actual play-back or recording. This takes a certain amount of time - between one and three seconds or more. But 25 to 75 frames will go by in one to three seconds.

The edit controller contains a memory chip, an EPROM, which knows how long your machines take. EPROMs can be programmed with data, and whoever manufactured your machines will probably have done so. (If not, you need to get in touch with the manufacturer and possibly even send your machines to them; they will then determine the data of your machines and program the EPROM with them.) Which brings us to the problem of editing precision...

Precision is Everything

You cut a photographic film with a pair of scissors or a splicer exactly in front of the desired cut-in point - that is, in front of a single frame; so you cut the film tape exactly at the point when, for example, a gust of wind blows your subject's hat off.

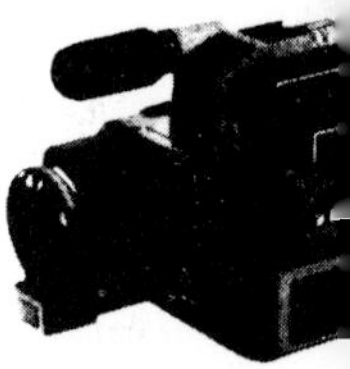

CAMCORDER OR PLAYER VIDEO 8

It is very difficult to achieve such precision in amateur video editing. This precision does not depend on the edit controller, either, but on the play-back and recording machines you use. In the Video 8 format the camcorder feeds the current counter position into the edit controller; it 'knows' this by counting the video tracks and also the pulses of the tape transport mechanism. Unfortunately 100% synchronization between the counter position and the single frame is not possible in this way; counting mistakes occur because of tape slippage during fast forward and rewind (when the camcorder is searching for the next scene). The editing displacement can be substantial when you're working roughly.

For example, you load a full 90-minute tape into the camcorder; you then select a scene at the very end, then one towards the beginning, next one towards the back, and so forth.

Controlled from the edit controller, the poor camcorder has to wind the tape from almost the beginning to almost the end, and back again; it almost gets hot in the process.

By the time you get to the fifth, sixth or seventh edits, they will be so far out (20 frames or more) from the frames you selected as the cut-in and cut-out points that you won't recognize the bit you wanted.

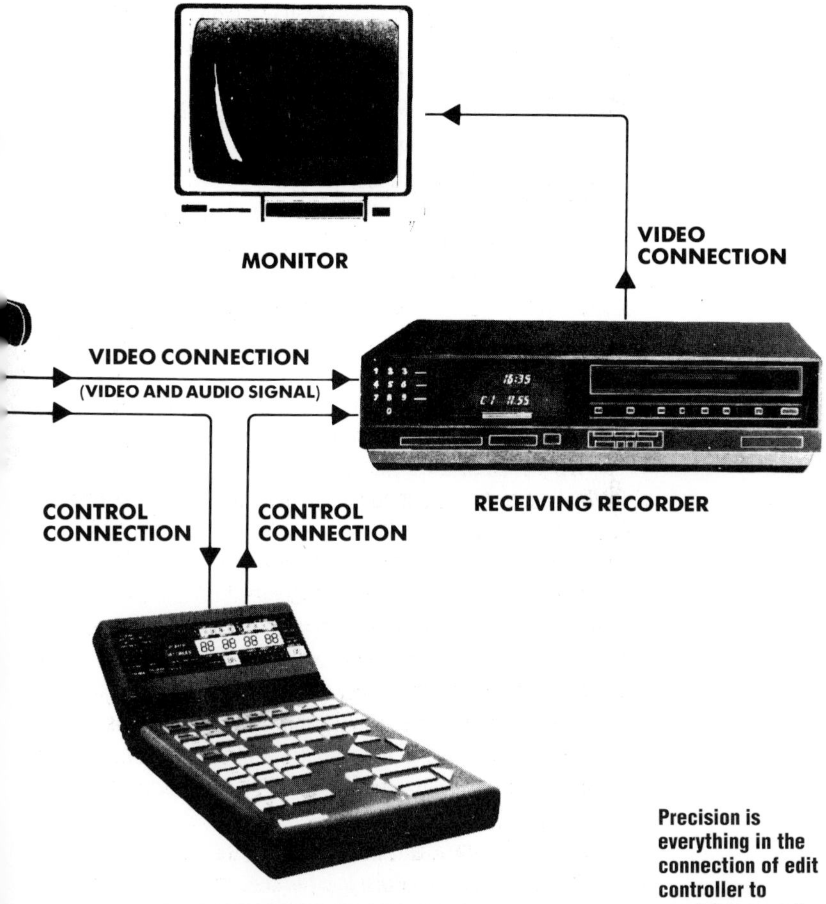

Precision is everything in the connection of edit controller to receiving recorder and camcorder.

Editing displacement therefore depends on how often you use the fast wind functions; in other words, it depends on how many edits need to be carried out and how far apart the cut-in and cut-out points are on the tape. There is only one remedy: input as few edits as possible at any one time, especially if the scenes are far apart.

Improvement with Time Code

It is, however, quite possible that editing precision in the Video 8 system will be improved dramatically in the foreseeable future - by means of the time code system. This is already used in professional Video 8 machines, and the VHS family has already introduced it into the amateur film-maker market.

Time code means that each single frame is given a unique number, consisting of the hour, minute and a frame number between 00 and 24. This number, which clearly identifies a single frame, is written onto the tape together with the video (image) and audio (sound) signals - in coded form, of course. Tape slippage therefore no longer matters because the information is recorded on the tape itself.

During play-back the frame numbers are fed into the edit controller where they are read by the decoder and displayed on the indicator panel. By pressing the correct buttons you can mark these numbers as either cut-in or cut-out points. In Preview mode and during the editing process itself, the play-back machine searches for the frame numbers of the frames which were selected as cut-in and cut-out points. If the pre-roll times of the machines are also right, you can cut precisely almost down to the single frame.

In Europe, the Videocut 10 Plus edit controller does not yet work with time code, but it is famous for the performance it can deliver, and is tuned for Video 8 and Video Hi-8 camcorders (as play-back machine). Its manufacturer claims an editing precision of +/- 6 frames, depending on the recorder.

Any video recorder of the VHS, S-VHS, Video 8, Video Hi-8 and Beta systems can be used as the recording machine.

With the Videocut 10 Plus you can pre-programme up to 100 scenes (cut-in and cut-out points); a large liquid crystal display

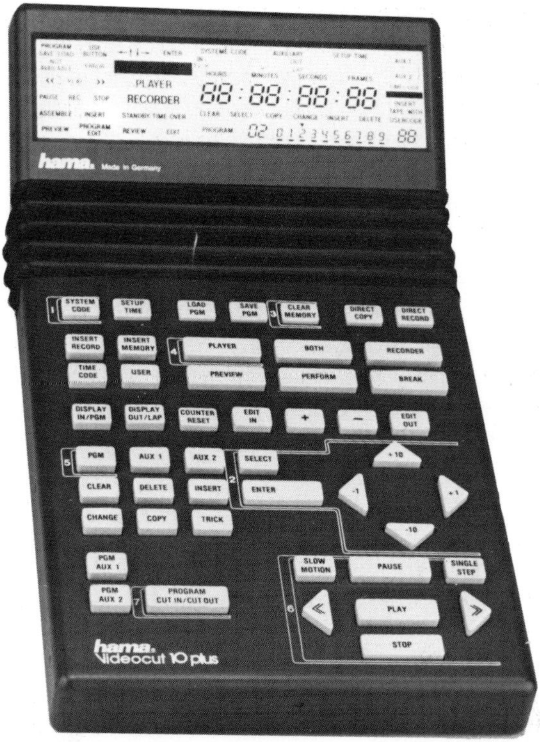

You can pre-programme up to 100 different scenes (cut-in and cut-out points) with the Videocut 10 Plus.

panel with 32 fields serves as the operating panel. The LCD panel shows all important data, such as scene length, overall duration of the edited scenes, or the current operating mode. All functions of the camcorder (play-back machine) necessary for editing are controlled by means of the generously-sized buttons of the Videocut 10 Plus, as are the cut-in and cut-out commands.

When you have finished editing a programme, you can store it on an audio compact cassette (the necessary connection socket/jack is built in) and re-use it at any time.

Many tricks are built in, for example the automatic repetition of scenes, or editing in a certain frame as a still image. The edit controller also has a socket/jack for connecting the Videoscript 55 title generator.

The Videocut 10 Plus learns the command codes of the video recorder used during the setting up process of the machine; a cable connection (for which the video recorder may not even have a socket/jack) is therefore not necessary for command transmission; instead, you simply place the infrared diode in front of the infrared sensor of the video recorder. The pre-roll times of a huge number of camcorders and video recorders are stored in the memory.

Tricks for Intermediate Edits and Titles

According to a well-known TV director "you find out where you've gone wrong during filming when you start cutting". Unfortunately not many amateurs - nor professionals - can jet back to the Maledives for every slip-up or missing scene - it's just too expensive. But you can often make do with tricks. Many an abrupt scene change or missing intermediate edit can be ironed out elegantly with a trick. Video processors are available for this purpose at moderate prices. GSE's AVEP-2s video processor is an example - quite a powerful one - of such processors. It offers the facility of correcting and transforming the colours of video shots. In addition, it is a multi-channel audio mixer, and it also contains an effects generator which enables you to break down images into different subjects and blend them in with wipe effects. You can also punch in colour frames. The AVEP-2s can process both the traditional CBVS and the Highband video signals.

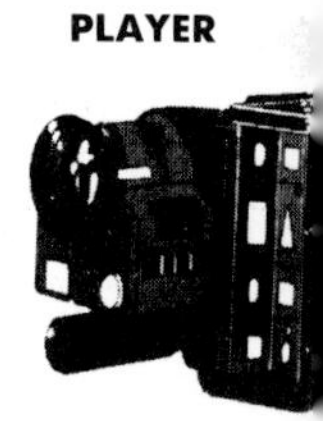

A really complete video does, of course, need titles, and very versatile title generators are available for this purpose. They can, for instance:

- fade in titles in eight colours and with more than 100 letters, numbers and symbols; these can also be reproduced as negatives, with the video image visible behind the symbols;
- simultaneously storing up to ten title pages with nine lines of twenty characters each;
- smooth fading, for example from the colour area to the image, or from the image to the colour area.

Talking of fading: every discriminating video amateur will sooner or later hit on the brilliant idea to connect two video recorders or camcorders with a third. When he's managed that, he will try to mix the images of the two play-back machines, or fade from one to the other. It doesn't work like this, can't work like this, because amateur video recorders can't be synchronised externally. The consequences are severe picture break-up. There is only one possibility: fade out from one video recorder, switch the second one to play-back and fade in.

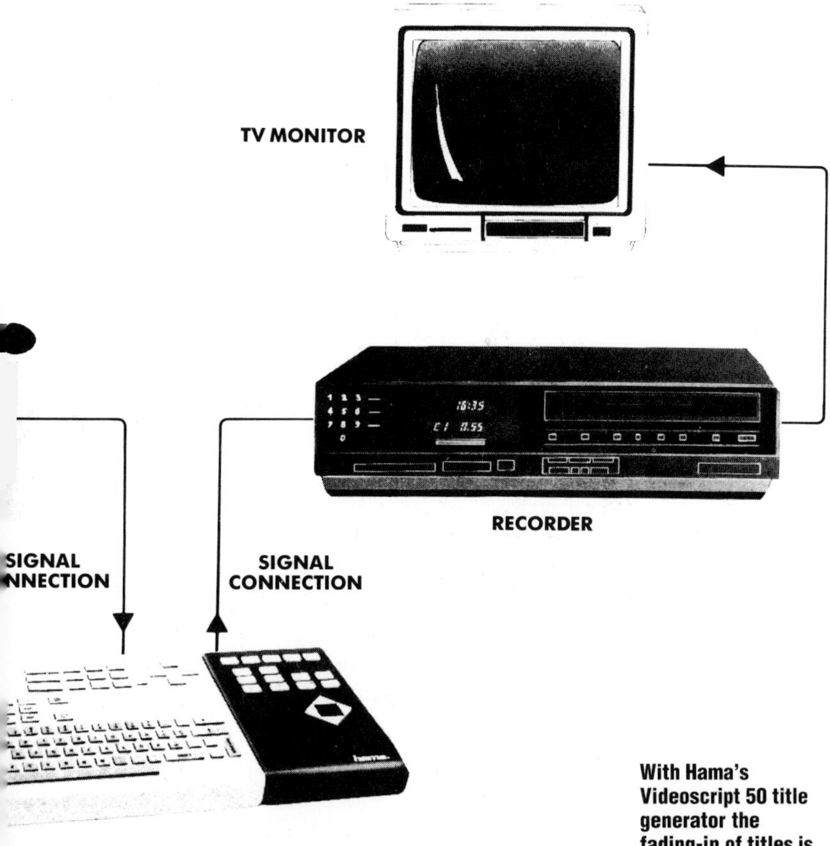

With Hama's Videoscript 50 title generator the fading-in of titles is possible without any problems.

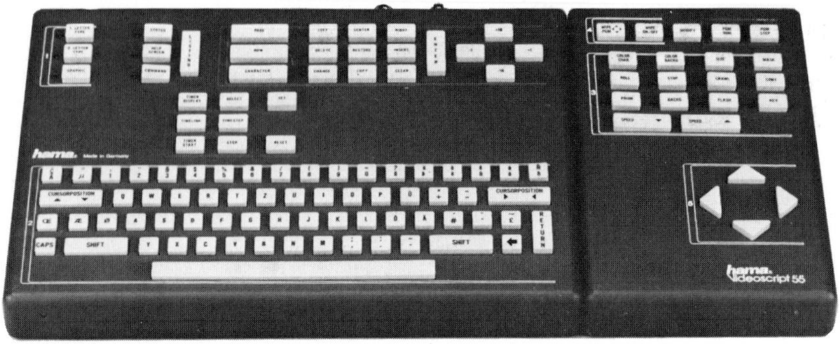

The Hama Videoscript 55 - a title and trick generator with remote control for all video equipment.

You will still get the break-up effect, but it is now in the fade and therefore not so noticeable.

When buying edit controllers, processors and mixers you really should seek advice from sales personnel in specialist shops who are familiar with them. Experts with top credentials can also be found in some amateur video clubs or video courses at evening classes. After all, editors, processors and mixers are, strictly speaking, specialized computers. Do read the more serious magazines for guidance as to different models available.

Talking of computers: videos and computers are coming increasingly close together. Feeding real shots into the computer as digitalized information and then re-working them with tricks, or generating whole videos with computers is now possible for amateurs, not only for only for professionals.

However sophisticated the machines are, they are like computers in that they don't do anything by themselves. From excitedly unpacking the machine and connecting everything together to the first successful video you have to gather your own experiences, and you can often end up working up a sweat. But what kind of boring hobby is one that doesn't cause any difficulties at all?

Photos and Films on Video

Moving pictures with dialogue and music are, of course, the great strength of video. But occasionally it is also desirable or necessary to integrate photos into the video film, or to transfer old Super 8 movies to video. Photos could be required for a linking edit, for example, or for a title or the final credits. Some people want to record their photo albums on video because it is easier for several people to look at photographs when they are on the TV monitor, and also because slide shows normally require too much effort in setting up.

Transferring paper prints causes the least problems. They are simply filmed. But you need to ensure correct lighting - reflections on the shiny surface of photographs can often interfere with the film. It is best to mount the camcorder on a repro stand and to work with a light source positioned at the side. Transferring transparent images - slides or negatives - is not quite so simple. However, slide adaptors for camcorders are available as accessories. They are suitable for 35mm slide or negative film and are simply attached to the front of the camcorder lens and lit from the front. There is nothing really wrong with this, except that the intrusive hot spot - the bright spot often produced by the light source in the centre of the image - should be prevented if possible. This hot spot also appears when projected slides or Super 8 movies are simply filmed from the screen or from special projection discs.

The new types of slide video projectors are a very expensive option of transferring slides to video. They resemble the traditional slide projectors, but have a CCD image sensor built in instead of the lens.They do deliver good quality, but are only suitable for framed 35mm slides. If you want to record slides or negatives on video, you need to work with a very precise trim at the image edge if the shot is to fill the TV monitor. This is because of the different proportions of the TV screen image and the 35mm format. Whereas the sides of a

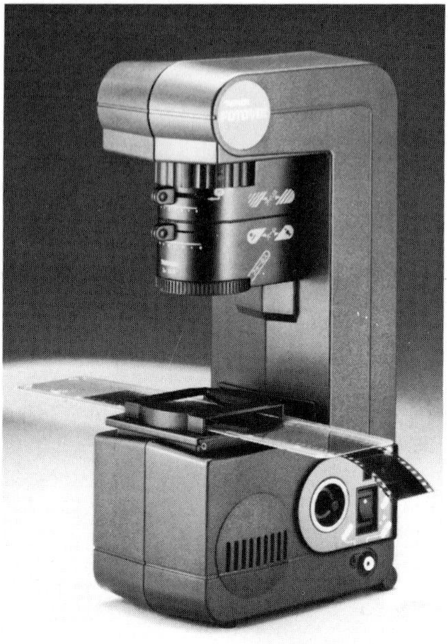

35mm shot are at a ratio of 2:3, it is 4:3 on the TV monitor. The most versatile device for transferring photographs to video is Tamron's Fotovix. This device with an integral video camera can be switched to positive or negative mode and can transfer slides as well as negatives onto video. It can also transfer sections of the slides. The zoom lens allows the image section to be altered. In addition, you can vary brightness and colour according to your own taste. A position regulator always places the shot in the right position on the monitor. Shots which are incorrectly placed or upside down can be placed correctly with a simple movement. It is equipped with a turning device for this purpose; this enables the image to be turned by 270° and also allows portrait shots to be inserted. A wide range of accessories include interchangeable lenses, converter elements and a device for automatic slide feeding. Images can be re-worked with the Fotovix Editor which can add frames, masks and markings to the shots. It can also be used to create wipe effects in numerous variations for transitions.

The Tamron Fotovix is a convenient device for copying slides, negatives and paper prints onto video.

The Telescreen Video is a simple device for transferring cine films onto video. The image is projected onto a 65x85mm matt screen and reproduced the right way around by means of a mirror. The image can then be filmed easily with a camcorder positioned in front of the translucent screen.

Good Connections and Hookups

Sockets/Jacks, Plugs and Adaptors

When you get home with your camcorder and you've taken really good shots, you and your family/relatives/friends won't just want to watch the result of your endeavours on the tiny black-and-white monitor of the camcorder, but on the large TV screen. So you need to find a way of sending the video (image) and audio (sound) signals from the camcorder to the TV set.

You can't play back Video 8 or Video Hi-8 cassettes in a VHS home recorder, and hardly anyone has a Video 8 format home recorder. So you have to connect the Video 8 or Video Hi-8 camcorder directly to the colour TV set.

Television Connection

There are basically two possibilities. One is a connection via the aerial cable, also called the RF connection (you will shortly see why). This has a big advantage: it works all the time, everywhere and with every TV/video recorder/camcorder, also with every VHS video recorder and camcorder, provided

● the machines work in the same colour TV standard; in Britain this is CCIR-PAL, in the USA it is NTSC. (If your camcorder has an RF converter with a G/I switch you will be able to play-back through another TV using the PAL system, i.e. Germany);

● your TV set is one of the new, high-quality, multi-standard machines; these can process any of the TV standards used throughout the world.

This connection via the aerial socket is called an RF connection because the UHF modulator that comes with the camcorder translates the video frequency into a frequency in the UHF band (Ultra High Frequency), to a channel between 30 and 40. However, this is not very convenient: you have to tune one of the TV's channel positions to the channel of the UHF modulator. It is important to select the channel position intended by the manufacturer (see the operating manual of the TV set).

Why? Every camcorder and video recorder produces time faults during play-back of a cassette. These cause the upper half of the image on the TV monitor to shift to the right, or shake violently. A time control device is located behind the channel position - many TV sets offer several - intended for the video recorder/camcorder. This device smooths out time fault fluctuations so that you can watch an acceptable picture.

The second disadvantage of the RF connection: it often doesn't reach maximum image quality. This is because (an increasing number of) terrestrial TV stations broadcast in UHF frequency. If a TV station works in the same frequency as the UHF modulator of your camcorder, its signal will interfere with your picture. This also happens if both UHF modulators of two connected video machines work in the same frequency. However, the frequency of a UHF modulator can be adjusted by carefully turning a small screw.

If you have a camcorder or video recorder with stereo sound, you should also avoid using the RF connection; 99.9% of RF modulators are designed as one-channel devices, so you will lose the stereo character. There is a further reason why the RF connection is not sufficient: if you are copying your cassette and want to control the transfer, you will need the aerial socket to connect the recording machine and TV set. The play-back recorder therefore has to be connected to the recording machine via the AV (Audio/Video) connection which is a technically superior type of connection anyway; it sends the video/audio (image/sound) signals into the TV set without the detour via the RF modulator and the reception component of the TV set.

Types of Connections and Hookups

This is where the problem of different plugs and sockets/jacks crops up. The whole thing only seems complicated here because we are describing all imaginable possibilities; but you at home will normally only have one camcorder, one video recorder and a TV set, so it all becomes a lot clearer.

First a word on the small but important difference, otherwise you're guaranteed to buy the wrong thing: the difference between plugs (male) and sockets/jacks (female):

- Equipment always has sockets/jacks.
- A cable with plugs (of whatever type) at both ends is called a coupling or copying cable.
- There are also couplers or connecters with sockets/jacks at both ends.
- A cable with a plug at one and a socket/jack at the other end is called an extension.
- If you want to connect two (or more) machines to one input or output port, you will need a distributor, which can, but does not have to be, a small box.

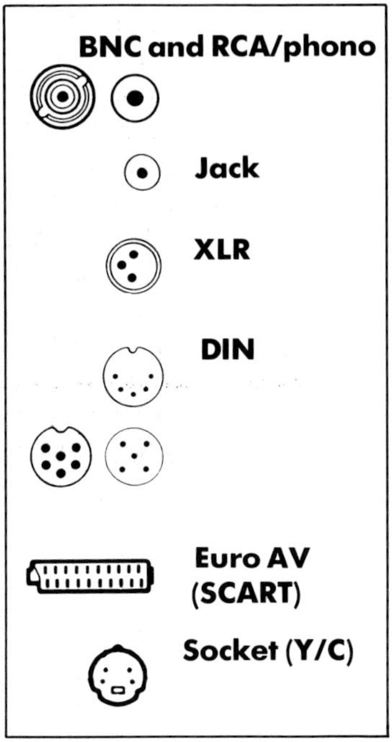

The different plugs and sockets/jacks enabling the connection from camcorder to TV set, and vice versa, can be confusing.

The sockets/jacks on the camcorder for the video (image) and audio (sound) signals are nearly always RCA/phono sockets/jacks (disregarding Video Hi-8 camcorders for the time being). This is the reason why cables with RCA/phono plugs are usually included in camcorder packages: one cable for the video (image), one for the audio (sound) - or, if it is a camcorder with stereo sound, one for the video (image), two for the audio (sound). RCA/phono sockets/jacks as video and audio input and output ports are becoming increasingly common on TV sets.

High-quality modern sets in Europe often have the sockets/jacks underneath a flap at the front which makes connection much easier. In the USA these are found on the side or rear.

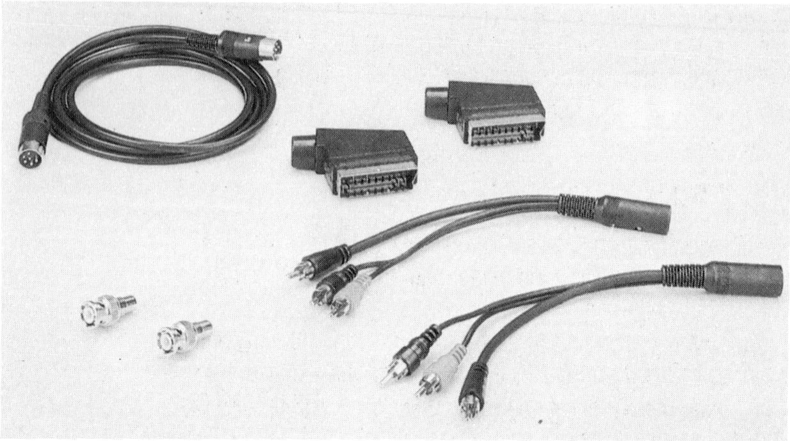

A universal video transfer recording set for play-back and recording (stereo) in both directions is available from many quality suppliers.

In Europe, manufacturers often include only the 21-pole EURO-AV socket as AV input/output socket; this is also called a SCART socket or (less frequently) EURO connector.

In older European TV sets (pre-1984) you will find the 6-pole DIN-AV socket as the AV input/output port. So what sort of an adaptor do you need? A Phono-to-SCART or Phono-to-DIN-AV adaptor. On older TV sets you also need to supply the SCART or DIN-AV socket with a 12 volt switch voltage. This has the following reason: when you switch on an older TV set it will show a picture from the TV transmitter. But we want to watch our video film, and this is where the trouble starts. Whoever set the standard for the DIN-AV and EURO-AV socket only thought about those video recorders which produce a 12 volt switch voltage when set to Play-back. This is fed into the TV set via the DIN-AV or the EURO-AV cable; this then switches off the TV picture and shows the picture from the video recorder.

But the camcorder doesn't produce the switch voltage, and it doesn't have an output port for it; the older TV set therefore doesn't switch off the TV transmitter and you can't watch your video. (On newer TVs you can switch off the tuner at the touch of a button, usually even via remote control.) The solution: there are special adaptors with small mains parts which provide the 12 volt switch voltage and deliver it to the correct pole of the DIN-AV or EURO-AV socket, and everything is O.K.

Copying

Of course you don't just want to watch your videos but also copy them in order to give a copy to friends, or to eradicate faults from the video during recording.

For this purpose the camcorder has to be connected to your home video recorder. It doesn't matter if the camcorder and video recorder work with different cassettes, such as Video 8 and VHS or VHS-C; the signals which go from one set of sockets/jacks into the other set are standardised. But they need to work in the same colour television system.

The home video recorder then has to be connected to the TV set so that you can preview what is being copied. You can use the RF connection for this purpose. A lot of what was said about the connection of camcorder and TV set also applies here:

- Older video recorders have DIN-AV sockets/jacks.
- Newer models in Europe have SCART sockets/jacks.
- New high-quality ones have RCA/phono or BNC sockets/jacks in addition to the SCART socket/jack, in the best cases even at the front. BNC is mostly used for the video (image) signal. BNC is very popular because it has optimum characteristics in both mechanical (because of the bayonet connection) and electrical terms.

The transition from BNC to RCA/phono and vice versa is simple: you attach a small adaptor piece (BNC-to-RCA/phono or RCA/phono-to-BNC). To get back to the camcorder-home recorder connection: two things are different from the earlier description of the connection of camcorder and TV set:

- The RF connection is now needed to connect the home recorder to the TV set, which serves as the control monitor.
- The home video recorder generally has to be switched to the AV input to which the camcorder is connected manually, by means of the input selection switch. It has to be set to external (line).

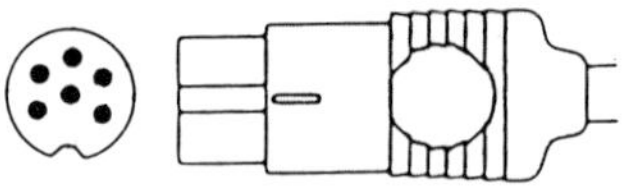

6-Pole DIN Plug

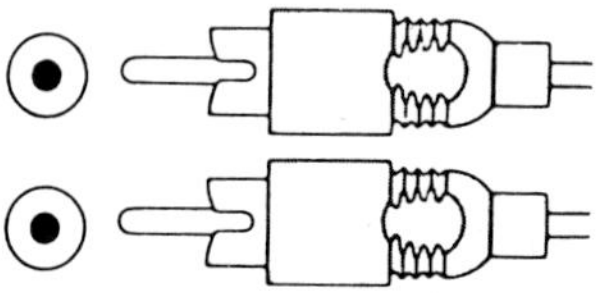

RCA/phono plugs

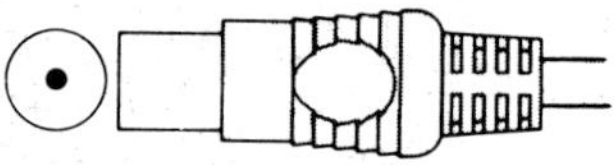

9.5mm Coaxial Plug

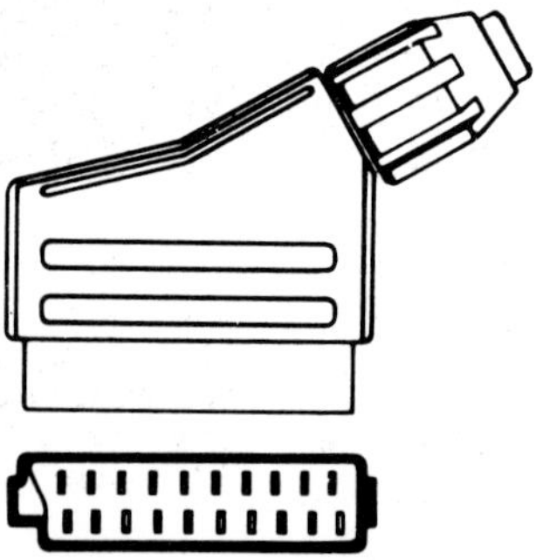

21-pole video plug, Scart

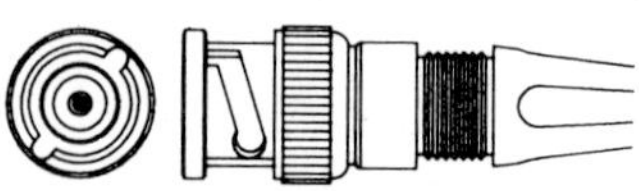

BNC video plug

If you then:

- switch on the camcorder, load a recorded cassette and start play-back, and
- the switched-on home video recorder is set to AV input - sometimes called Ext (for external) or line - and
- the correct channel is selected on the TV set;

You will see your video recordings on the monitor and hear the sound from the TV loudspeaker. All you then need to do is load a blank tape into the video recorder, and you can start copying or editing.

Top class camcorders, that is Video Hi-8 camcorders, can be connected in the same way (see above) as all other camcorders:

- in the RF way via the aerial cable, and
- via the AV cable (Hi-8 camcorders sometimes have RCA/phono AV sockets/jacks which carry the composite video signal and the audio signal).

But you won't get the maximum image quality High Band camcorders are capable of in this way. Their real strength lies in the separate processing of the brightness and colour signals. In order to get the high resolution and colour purity, these signals also have to be fed into the colour TV set separately.

The same applies if you even have an S-VHS or Hi-8 home recorder and want to copy onto it. For this purpose the Video Hi-8 camcorder has an S-socket/jack, which is also called a Y/C socket/jack. And your colour TV set, too, needs to have such a socket/jack.

Whereas High Band camcorders come with the Y/C socket/jack - the small, round, 4-pole S-socket/jack - there are two different types of sockets/jacks on the colour TV set:

● either the above-mentioned S-socket/jack, or;

● (in Europe) a second SCART socket which can be switched to Y/C signals.

High-quality modern colour TV sets have both sockets/jacks. Manufacturers supply S-cables with their High Band camcorders; depending on the company philosophy, these either have S-plugs at both ends, or adaptors.

Most recently some companies (Hitachi, for example) have started to install a special socket/jack for Y/C audio signal in their High Band camcorders; the corresponding connection cable is included. 2-pole or 3-pole jack plugs and the corresponding socket(s)/jack(s) are typical inputs and outputs for microphones and earphones (the 3-pole version is for stereo sound). These plugs and sockets/jacks usually have a diameter of 3.5mm, less frequently one of 2.5mm; adaptors for this norm are widely available.

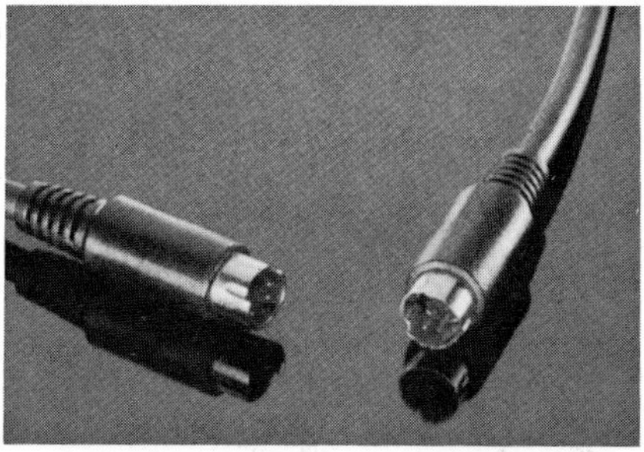

A so-called S-plug, also called a Y/C plug, is required for the transfer of an S-VHS signal.

The 2.5 or 3.5 jack plug can sometimes be found on cable remote controls which simply serve for switching on and off (or Start/Stop). So in this case they are used to conduct direct current. Coaxial (coax for short) plugs and sockets/jacks, usually serve to connect the mains/charging device and the camcorder required for play-back and for editing and copying.

Re-working, that is editing and post sound recording, is very popular. To make this as easy as possible, many camcorders have a special Edit cable connection; this cable can then be plugged into the Edit socket/jack of the home video recorder (if it has one). If everything is connected correctly, camcorder play-back and video recorder recording start simultaneously at the touch of a button (on the camcorder).

There are attempts to standardise the Edit sockets/jacks and cables, but no standard has yet become accepted, and you therefore need to get the relevant cable from one of the manufacturer's service agents.

Finally: a few tips, if you want to buy adaptors and cables, you should:

- carefully examine the machines you want to connect at home;
- make outline drawings of the required sockets, and
- of the signal paths.

Don't rush into the shop and take the first thing you see, otherwise you'll probably grab the wrong blister pack (cables and adaptors mostly hang on racks in the accessory corner). You have to be particularly careful with Euro SCART adaptors: in order to save money and weight only the poles needed for a certain connection are usually connected by a one-way cable; a fully-connected two-way SCART cable is as thick as a thumb.

This is why you need to look carefully at the wiring diagram printed on the blister pack - and, most important, ask a knowledgeable salesperson - otherwise the signal will never get to the pole it is supposed to.

When you have finished connecting everything but cannot see your camcorder picture on your TV, carefully check over all the cables and settings, working from the camcorder through to the TV. You will usually have everything working properly second time around.

It is arguable whether plugs should be gold-plated, but you will undoubtedly get into terrible trouble with super-cheap cables and adaptors: a single sloppy soldered joint, one bad contact, and you can forget copying altogether. If you are buying a new TV set and/or a new video recorder, you should make sure you don't end up with a model from the Stone Age; as a video film-maker you will get far more pleasure from a modern machine that will give you maximum facilities when you connect it to your camcorder.

Adding Appropriate Sound

A movie, however well-directed, would not have the same impact without suitable sound.

The Hollywood movie *Earthquake* sets the cinema audience's teeth on edge; it bombards us with frequencies barely audible because they are too low for the human ear, but played with such power that they almost makes our stomachs vibrate. In short: moving images only become a film when sound is added.

The fact that movies used to be silent is no argument for silence. In the old silent cinema a pianist did his best during each performance to add emotion to the silent movie. Music has contributed substantially to many a film's success. Just think of Scott Joplin's ragtime in *The Sting*, the helicopter attack accompanied by *Ride of the Valkyries* in *Apocalypse Now*, or the theme tune of *The Good, the Bad and the Ugly*.

"Moving images only become a film when sound is added, and music has contributed substantially to many a film's success"

A video film, too, is incomplete without sound, like a painting without a frame. On the other hand, sound can intensify the effect of a video tremendously. The following amateur video remains unforgettable for me and many friends. A Japanese garden in the rain; a small temple; a few visitors are standing or sitting silently; the film-maker records the silent, but concentrating people - mostly in 2/3 length or faces - and later adds a classical European tune (Mozart from the Walkman he has brought along). The atmosphere, the music - fascinating! The panel of judges in the competition unanimously awarded first prize to it.

Sound - the Poor Relation

Why are we describing it in such detail? The reason is that sound is still a real problem in amateur video filming. There are reasons of course. On the one hand, every camcorder has an integral microphone, and every camcorder records the sound at every film location by itself, synchronised and controlled fully automatically.

But on the other hand, for this very reason - the fact that it all happens as a matter of course - nobody bothers with sound and gives away incredible opportunities. The video industry estimates the proportion of video film-makers paying attention to sound to be two to five per cent.

Numerous manufacturers offer external microphones with different directional characteristics as accessories for camcorders.

And thirdly: it needs to be said that it is much easier to record good images on location than good sound. It is also true to say that reworking sound with amateur equipment is extremely difficult. Something which works at the touch of a button in a film sound studio is basically completely impossible with amateur equipment.

Therefore beware of wishful thinking: perfect video sound is hopelessly out of the video film amateur's reach, however keen.

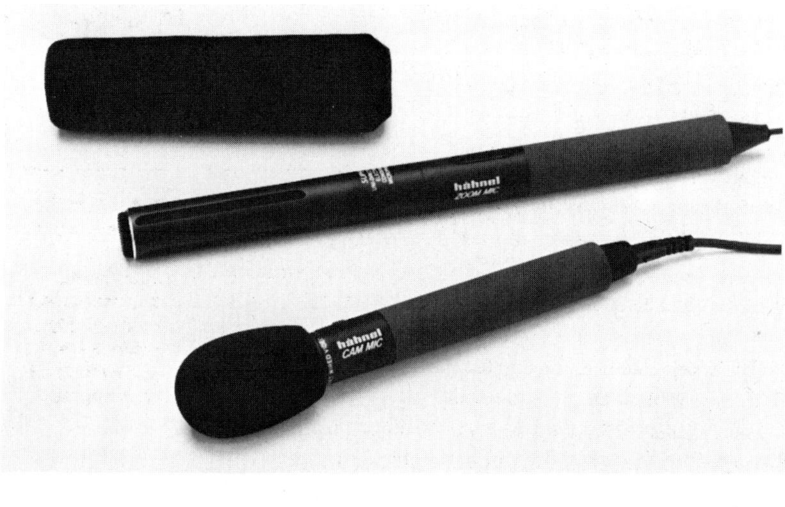

The Microphone

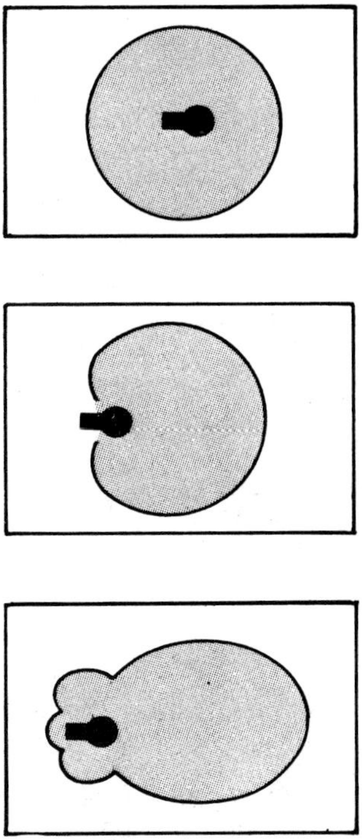

The schematic diagrams above show the directional characteristics of spheroid (top), cardioid (centre) and directional microphones.

Let's consider the issue from the very beginning, from the live recording on location. Our camcorder has an integral electret condenser microphone. (If you're interested in the technical aspect: inside the microphone is a membrane with an electric charge - hence the name electret. Pressure waves in the air - sound - cause the membrane to vibrate; this produces signals in a small, electrically conducting plate which is built in parallel with the membrane.) Such microphones are a good compromise in terms of size, price and performance.

On some camcorders the microphone is fairly sensitive to the noise of the camcorder mechanism, the autofocus and zoom motors, as well as operating noises (for example, the cameraman pressing a button). So you will hear a more or less pronounced sawing, buzzing and/or tapping during the recording. This also depends on where on the camcorder body the microphone is situated (the further away from sources of noise, the better), and how it is mounted (noise suppression measures). Test reports in good specialist magazines will give details of respective models' sensitivity to mechanism, zoom, autofocus and operating noises. In very small camcorders the microphone is usually fixed in the body, and therefore fairly sensitive to these problems.

Every microphone has certain characteristics. We talk about a spheroid characteristic if the microphone records sound from all directions with almost the same intensity. A microphone with a cardioid characteristic records sound coming from the front more strongly than that coming from behind; this frontal orientation is even stronger on the super-cardioid, and strongest on the directional microphone. Most camcorder microphones have a cardioid characteristic. This means:

- If the cameraman breathes loudly, talks or even shouts directions during filming, those sounds will be recorded fully on the soundtrack.

● Nowadays amateur camcorders come with long telephoto focal lengths: 6x, 8x or even 12x zooms, not to mention interchangeable lenses and telephoto lens converters. If you are working with a telephoto focal length, the image size and acoustic distance will no longer agree. After all, you are only recording the sound around the camcorder, and not the sound coming from the subject. The sound doesn't zoom with the lens.

Take for example, an idyllic lake in the evening sunshine; you are filming a sailing boat gliding along on the lake; next to you your wife, girlfriend or kids are chatting away happily. Their chatter will be on the soundtrack, ruining everything.

Another sound problem often arises in interviews; on recordings with the camcorder microphone it is difficult or impossible to understand what the interviewees are saying, and with close-up shots their voices sound very far away. The opposite problem can arise with close-up and macro shots: you are filming a beautiful hibiscus blossom to fill the frame, and 40-ton trucks are thundering past behind your back - it will all be on the soundtrack.

"If we want to record good sound we need to learn to hear like a camcorder microphone"

In general you will notice how acoustically polluted our environment is when you watch and consciously listen to your recordings. The microphone hears what we have stopped noticing: planes in the sky, the noise of motor traffic, the confusion of voices from all around. What does this tell us? If we want to record good sound we need to learn to hear in the same way as the camcorder microphone.

Wind is another serious problem. There is as yet no remedy for the whispering of the wind in the microphone; you can still hear it, despite wind filters which can be switched in and are integrated in more and more camcorders.

The fully automatic control of the sound recording level is welcomed by most amateur video film-makers: you don't need to worry about it.

But it also has its own drawbacks: the automatic control tends to a) hiss and b) pump. This means:

a) If only low sound reaches the microphone on location, the sound level control fully turns up the amplifier; the S/N, signal to noise, ratio becomes incorrect, and the sound recording hisses.

b) If there are several transient, substantially louder sounds (bangs) in the general sound level on location, the automatic control reduces the level every time with a certain delay, and then, again with a delay, brings it back to normal; the recording sound swells up and down unnaturally, in other words: it pumps.

So what can we do at least to partially solve these sound problems?

Only manual control of the sound recording can avoid this pumping of the automatic control; however, only high-quality (and relatively expensive) camcorders offer this facility. An external microphone can be connected to 99% of all camcorders. You can either simply pull out the integral microphone because it sits in a plain jack socket (with a diameter of 3.5 or 2.5mm - see operating manual); or an external microphone can be plugged into a separate jack socket.

This directional video microphone has a super-cardioid characteristic which mainly records sound reaching the microphone from the front.

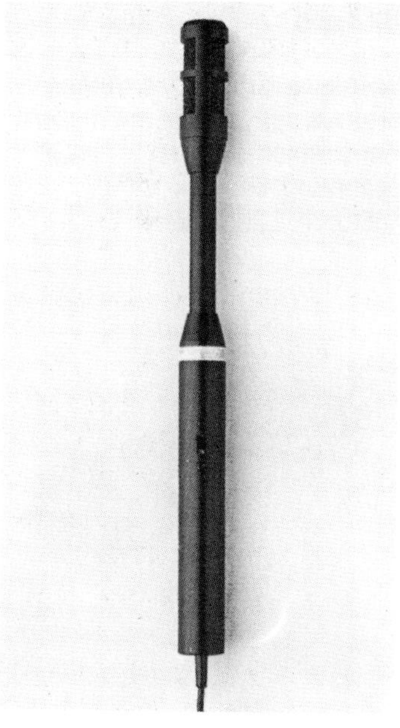

If the correct jack plug is plugged into the jack socket, the integral microphone is switched off. We should remember this, because it can help us get out of many a tight spot.

Camcorder manufacturers, as well as accessory manufacturers, offer a fairly wide range of external microphones for video filming:

● Microphones with substantially improved frequency modulation (also available in stereo versions); for better recordings of subjects like musical events;

● Microphones with long cables so that the mike can be brought closer to the sound source than the camcorder. This can be very useful, if you want to record an event happening on a stage - provided you manage to lay the cable in advance;

● Directional microphones with windbreaks;

● Microphones with parabolic mirrors (ultra-directional effect), which will help you get

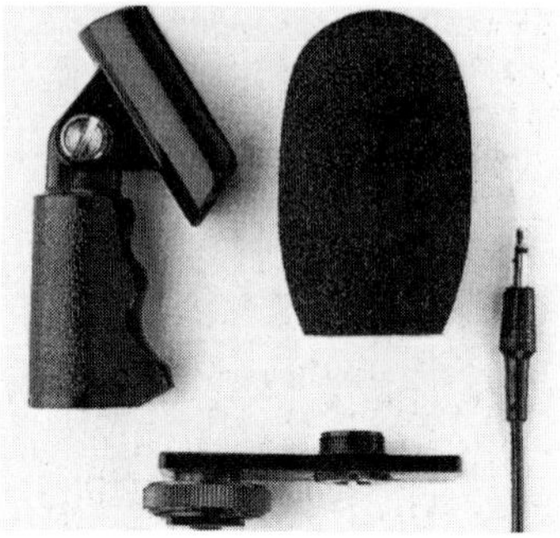

acoustically close to subjects like wild animals;

● Tiny personal microphones for interviews, or table microphones for similar uses;

● Underwater microphones for snorkling or diving.

But if all the measures mentioned don't help we have two choices:

1. We film without sound. On romantically idyllic shots (evening at the lake, hibiscus blossom) in particular, it is better to do without the original location sound if it destroys the mood captured on the image. So we film silently and add sound and/or appropriate music at home. How do you film silently? If the camcorder microphone can be pulled out, we pull it out; if it can be switched off, we switch it off; if neither is possible we get hold of a jack plug without a cable which fits into the socket/jack for the external microphone and plug it in - the integral microphone is then turned off.

Accessories for directional microphones: a spiral cable with a 3.5mm jack plug and a microphone holder.

2. We record the original sound separately, with a good sound recording device which is independent of mains supply, for example a Walkman, or better still, one of the new DAT recorders. But we have to destroy yet another illusion here: you will not manage to copy the original sound onto the edited video in synch later because today's amateur video machine and the amateur sound recorder cannot be synchronized. Professional equipment does do this but it's not affordable by amateurs.

Typical microphone accessories: adaptors, cables with jack plugs, wind protection, microphone holder and camera shoe.

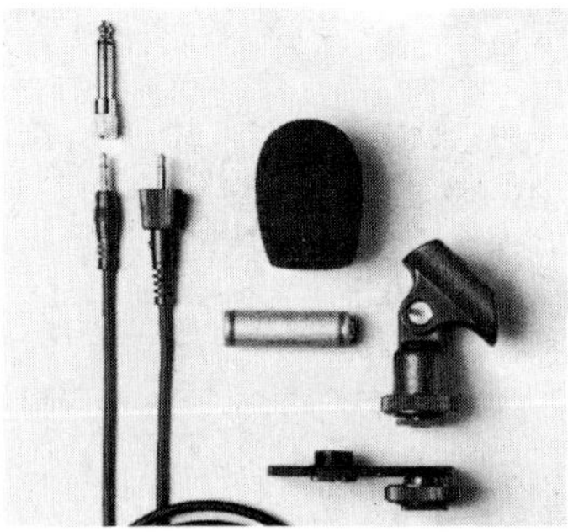

Synchronization becomes a huge problem in one special case of video filming: the recording of live music in the widest sense, which might be a jazz session in a pub, a carnival procession, a summer fete, or a college ball. Such events are often the highlights of the year in a town, club or school. The video film-maker can hardly refuse the categoric request from friends: 'You'll film it, won't you!'. Few tasks are more difficult. This is what normally happens: wedged into a throng of party-minded fellow human beings, the video fan tries to capture the musical performance. It will last three or five minutes, or even longer. After one or two minutes the cameraman is overcome by a deep sense of unease: the arm goes stiff. sweat stands out on the brow, the viewfinder eyepiece steams up, and the band has ceased to be visually interesting. Every face, every instrument has been filmed to the full - what now?

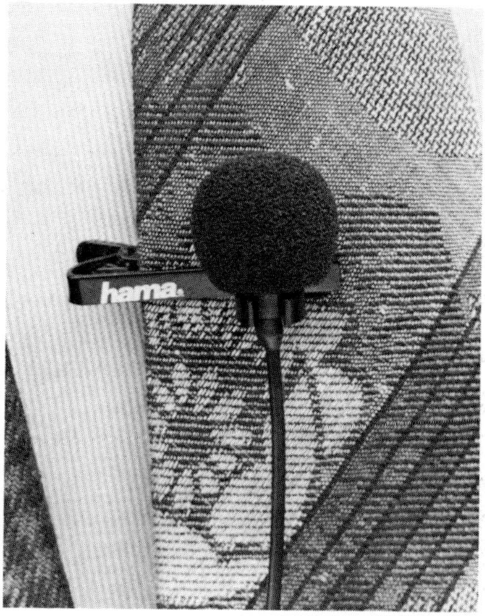

Convenient for interviews and commentary: tie microphones.

A change of position would be good. it would be nice to film intermediate shots of party guests. But how?

● If the cameraman starts marching off - provided the crowds let him - with the camera running, the picture will: a) be shaking madly and; b) have numerous unsharp parts.

● If he switches off the camcorder to change position, he will miss - irretrievably - a piece of the live music, and there will be abrupt jumps of sound at the editing points where he switched off and on: the previous and subsequent sound won't fit together. So what can you do? One possibility is to record with two (or more) camcorders simultaneously: one keeps on the band and films at least one full piece of music, more if possible. The second camcorder films the audience/party guests at the same time.

The tape with the band serves as the base; its sound recording runs through; from the other tape (tapes) you only take the shots, that is, the best bits, and edit them into the base tape as insert edits. This method has the advantage that image and sound are at least in synch while the musicians are in the shot.

The second possibility: you record the sound with a tape recorder. You edit the picture tape and add the music.

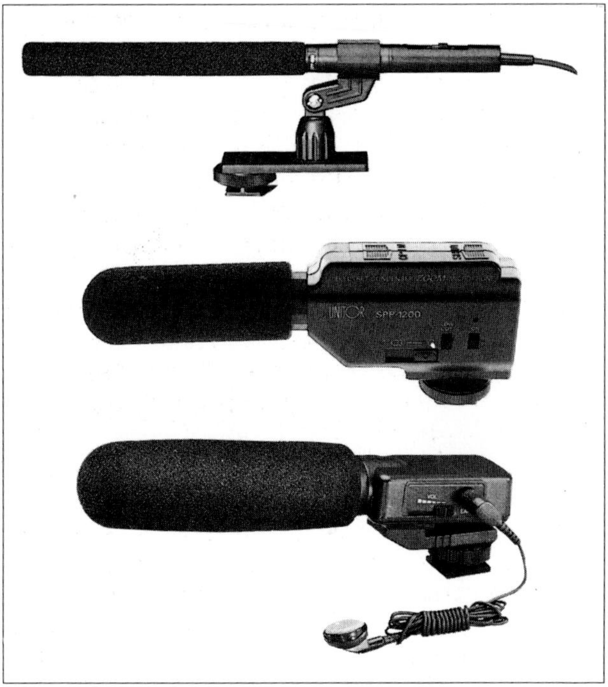

Good microphones are a prerequisite for good sound. The photograph shows the SPP 600 telescope microphone from Tokina (top), underneath the Zoom-Micro SP 1200 and the SP 1300 with integral amplifier.

Video and Sound not in Synch

But that is easier said than done, for as stated before, video and tape machine can't be synchronized. This means that if you start both the image and the sound tape at zero, an action in the image and its sound will no longer happen at the same time even after a few dozen seconds, let alone minutes. Image and sound are asynchronous, and people notice that immediately.

As an amateur you can't do anything about it, you can only cheat:

● Either you don't show the action very clearly in the image (that is, the drummer hitting the drum with the drumstick, the guitarist plucking the string, a spectator clapping his hands together),

● or you turn down the sharp sound and add a commentary, that is, distract the audience a little from the lack of synchonization.

An audio mixer with inputs for several sound sources (microphone, tape recorder, record player, CD player) and earphone output would come in very handy for this. If you have video equipment with stereo sound, the inputs need to be two-channel inputs. The chapter *Sockets/Jacks, Plugs and Adaptors* covers the connection of the sound output socket(s) of the audio mixer and the recording video machine (camcorder, home video recorder).

What does the audio mixer do? Let's pretend we're not very bright and put it like this: you can input several sound sources (see above), select the desired sound or sounds by moving the levers up and down, also create smooth transitions, influence the relative volume levels, check the mix over the earphones, talk over the sound live, and channel the entire mix to the output, whose level can once more be influenced by a lever.

With stereo audio mixers you can even influence the relationship between the left and right channel, or reverse the channels so that what came from the right now comes from the left. With some audio mixers you can even influence the frequency level; you can, for example, increase or decrease treble sections or bass sections.

Audio mixers are offered by many camcorder and accessory manufacturers at prices which are very affordable for the amateur market and in several performance classes. Some companies even combine the audio mixer with an image processor; and there is even a combined audio mixer/image processor/edit controller. Check a specialist video magazine to see the choice available.

In practice sound mixing means that you watch the image tape and push the right lever (with music, sound etc) at the right time, or speak your commentary into the mike.

This does, of course, require presence of mind and practice. If it all gets too hectic for you, you can record your mix onto an audio cassette first and then sound record the image tape later.

We have talked about post sound recording several times; unfortunately we are not spared the need to consider the technical aspects.

A Video 8 camcorder doesn't have longitudinal track sound recording; it records sound frequency-modulated (FM) on diagonal tracks with audio heads which are mounted on the rotating head drum. The tape speed no longer matters, only the relative speed

Audio mixers for stereo sound serve for the mixing together of different sources of sound, such as tape recorder, record player and microphone.

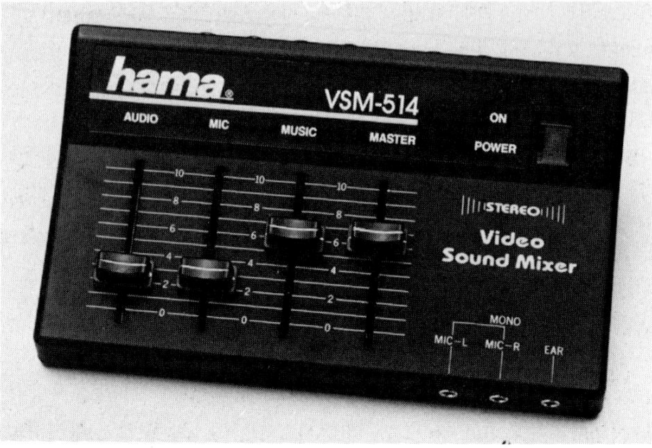

between the tape and the heads is important. This is 3.1 metres per second in Video 8 and Video Hi-8, which is faster than on a costly professional tape recorder (19 or 38 centimetres per second). Cheaper Video 8 camcorders record mono sound in hi-fi quality. More high-quality Video 8 camcorders also offer FM stereo hi-fi sound.

The audio (sound) and video (image) signals are inextricably linked together. Post sound recording without simultaneous re-recording of the image is therefore not possible directly in the camcorder. But the Video 8 developers came up with something else. The video and audio tracks in Video 8 are not written as long as they could be; a small section of the track remains empty at the top of every track, and hi-fi stereo sound in pulse code modulation (PCM) can be written onto this small section. Play-back almost reaches compact disc quality. The PCM sound written in this way is, of course, completely independent of the video signal; the PCM tracks can therefore be used for top quality post sound recording directly in the camcorder, whilst the original sound recorded on location is fully preserved on the diagonal tracks.

This PCM sound facility can be found on Video 8 recorders - though only on the top-quality, and therefore most expensive, examples of their type - as well as Video Hi-8 home recorders.

"PCM sound play-back almost reaches compact disc quality"

Let's assume you don't have a Video 8 or even Video Hi-8 home recorder, nor a Video 8 camcorder with PCM sound. What do you do? In this case, you have two choices:

● If your home recorder has an Audio Dubbing facility you copy your Video 8 tape onto a VHS tape and post sound record this.

● But you can also copy the Video 8 tape with the VHS home recorder: via the video lead; the new sound is added at the same time via the audio lead from the mixer or from an audio tape machine, onto which you have recorded your mix (see above).

If you have read this far you may have started to think and tell yourself: all this sound business and its re-working is quite a complicated process. And you'd be completely right. Perhaps you'll be comforted to know that even cinema films and TV programmes often fail because of their sound.

Sound engineers and assistants with the best training and years of experience are needed for sound recording and re-working.

It also requires a huge amount of equipment. On the one hand this equipment is very expensive, but on the other hand it can be synchronized externally: a central time-keeping device forces all video/audio recording and play-back machines to work in synch. Such machines are used, for example, by broadcasting authorities.

This means that if you start the video and audio tapes at zero (wherever the machines are physically situated), they will still be running in synch after several hours - the action in the picture exactly matches its sound on the soundtrack - if it doesn't, the machine's broken.

Something like this is not (yet) available on amateur equipment. Nobody should be under the illusion that producing a perfect video clip with music as on TV is within the means of the amateur. Editing to music - exactly on the beat, down to a sixteenth of a bar - doesn't work (yet) with amateur equipment. It is therefore all the more exciting for - near-expert - viewers if a keen amateur manages to produce a good edit and good post sound recording, despite all the difficulties described.

A hobby where you don't have to overcome any difficulties isn't a proper hobby. Why should a real mountaineer risk the difficult climb up the north face of the Eiger when he could take the Jungfrau-Joch train?

Tips, Tricks and Trouble-shooting

So here it is: the box containing the brand-new camcorder. Surrounded by an excited family you take the technical miracle from its packaging.

Here is a first tip: camcorder packaging isn't very bulky - please keep it all! You can take a vacuum cleaner, microwave, colour TV set etc. to a local specialist workshop without its packaging without much difficulty. But a camcorder almost always needs to be returned to the manufacturer should it need service. Its innards are too small and complicated for normal radio/TV mechanics, and special tools and test equipment are required for repair. If you despatch your camcorder without its tailor-made polystyrene packing you might see some damage. However, to start with you don't think about future repairs, of course. You happily handle the machine and want to start filming but you should always start by reading the operating manual.

"If you despatch your camcorder without its tailor-made polystyrene packing you might see some damage"

Operating manuals are funny things: many people seem mystified by them, but they cannot do without them:

● When you start using the camcorder you will see a number of messages and indications in the form of letters, figures and symbols in the viewfinder and, if available, on an LCD (Liquid Crystal Display) panel. You need to know what they mean, of course, and you'll find out from the operating manual.

● You have spent a lot of money on the features of your camcorder: high speed shutter, digital superimpose and perhaps title generators, trick features such as positive/negative switching; some camcorders even have automatic programmes which allow you to determine what your shots will look like - a deep or shallow depth of field, for instance, or as little movement blur as possible on sports shots, and so on. The operating manual will tell you how they are used and with what results.

We are about to tell you how the irritating study of the operating manual can become sheer pleasure; however, you should carry out the following before your first serious film work:

In a quiet hour, perhaps when you are at home alone with nobody to disturb you:

● prepare the camcorder for recording

● connect it to your TV set; you will also find out how this works, and whether the cable delivered with the camcorder fits into the socket/jack of your TV set, or whether you need adaptors;

● turn the volume of the TV set down to zero (otherwise you get a shrill whistling tone);

● put the operating manual in front of you, plus a piece of paper and a pen.

Now you can run through all the buttons, switches and features, as described in the operating manual, in peace and quiet. You should also pay attention to what the picture looks like, for example if you are recording in too little light, and what the effects are of daylight, artificial light and mixed light; what happens if you are working with the hand-held camera at the longest focal lengths (the picture is shaking like mad), and how long it takes the autofocus to focus if you are zooming quickly from wide-angle to telephoto. You will see the immediate effects of your actions on the TV set, and you should also watch the indications in the viewfinder monitor and LCD panel.

You are, of course, recording your experiments onto the tape (you can re-record it with new, proper recordings later), and note what you were doing at any one time; at the end you should watch the test tape carefully, consulting your notes. In the process you will become familiar with the camcorder, get a feel for handling it, know all the flashing indicators, and learn to use the features confidently.

These are the best conditions to prepare you for your first real shots.

You think this is too complicated? There is a different way - also very instructive, as you will see. You have inserted the battery pack into the battery compartment without looking in the operating manual; found the Power button for switching on and the Eject button to open the cassette compartment, into which you load a cassette. Off you go to film your first video. That's what you think. The viewfinder image stays black, and nothing is happening. Is the camcorder broken? Not at all. According to the customer services manager of a large camcorder manufacturer, statistics show that out of a thousand camcorders sold and in the original packaging no more than two or three will be faulty. No, the reason why the camcorder is not working is that the battery pack is discharged! The fact that the cassette compartment still opened is no proof it will work! All battery packs are delivered in the discharged state. The pack has to be charged for an hour or more before you can get the first shots on tape. That means - start again. Connect the battery charger to the mains socket and the camcorder. The cable is either permanently fixed to the charger or packed separately - have a look in the operating manual. However, keep in mind that filming and battery charging at the same time are not possible.

So what's wrong now? We've got a great picture in the viewfinder, but what about recording? It's possible that the camcorder is still not recording. You should have read the operating manual after all.

"All battery packs are delivered discharged. The pack has to be charged for an hour before the first shots can go on tape"

The camcorder consists of two machines: a colour video camera and a colour video recorder. The camera component converts light into signals which the recorder can record onto magnetic tape and play back later. So you have to switch to what you want: video filming or play-back. On many camcorder models the on/off button is a slide switch which has three positions: Camera for video film recording, Off (the power is then switched off) and VCR (short for Video Cassette Recorder) for play-back.

If the switch is set to VCR, different buttons (which are often hidden under a flap) from those used in Camera mode are responsible for the camcorder's operation. So the switch has to be set to Camera for video filming.

On other camcorder models the on/off button only has those two settings. The camcorder then remembers the operating mode which was selected when the camcorder was switched off; when it is switched on again it will start in the operating mode selected previously. You can switch to Camera by means of the Stop button (one of the buttons specifically used in VCR mode).

You're finally ready: the charged battery pack is in its compartment, a cassette without record protect is in the cassette compartment.

Record protect? What's that? On Video 8 and Video Hi-8 cassettes it is a small slide switch at the back of the tape which is used to prevent a recorded cassette being re-recorded, erasing the previous

Most tapes can be protected against accidental erasing through re-recording by breaking off the record protect tab. Some manufacturers also use the slide switches shown in this diagram.

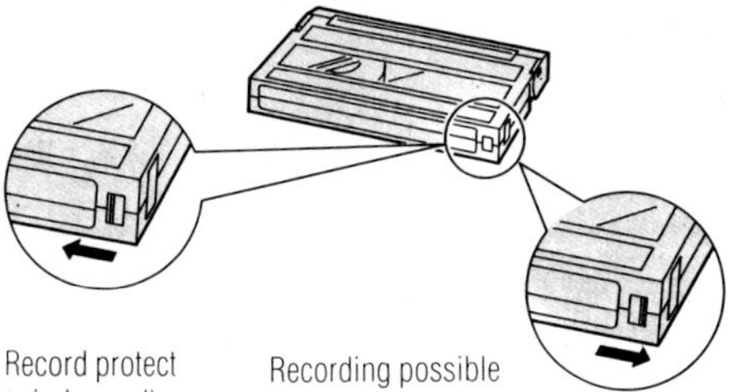

recording. If a small red area is visible, the switch is in the Protect position; a black area means recording is possible.

So, the battery pack and cassette are in, the camcorder switched on and set to Camera: are we now ready to roll?

Perhaps not: if you can only see a sort of white snowstorm in the viewfinder you have left the lens cap on. But the lens cap is important.

1. Always put it on the lens when you are not recording. In this way you protect the front element against dust and greasy fingerprints.

A lens cap is even more important when you are close to salt water. Dried salt water splashes are almost impossible to get off the front element, and its coating can be damaged. If salt water does get on the front element - during filming, for example - wipe it off with a lens cloth immediately; whatever you do, don't let it dry!

Here is another reason why the lens caps needs to go on the lens: if sun-rays enter through the unprotected lens, it has the effect of a magnifying glass, the image converter (CCD) chip gets very hot and is damaged, and you'll end up with a very expensive repair job.

2. When you take off the lens cap it dangles from a short piece of cord. If there is more than a gentle breeze it can dangle in front of the lens and therefore in front of the picture. The remedy: most lens caps have a clip with which they can be fastened to the hand loop - and you really should do this.

3. A milky white disc can be found inside some lens caps: it is used for manual white balance.

Right, now we can start filming. And there won't be any problems to start with because the camcorder has automatic programmes for everything:

● One sets the sharpness (autofocus).

● The second controls the amount of light reaching the image converter (aperture control or automatic exposure control, AE for short).

● If the amount of light is very low, the automatic gain control ensures that you will get a picture, although it may contain a certain amount of pale, unnatural colours.

● The third programme ensures that - at a normal amount of light - the colours are nice and natural (white balance, or WB for short).

So the video film-maker doesn't need to worry about anything, just press the start/stop button (which is located on the handgrip and is often red).

Now you will probably make a typical beginner's mistake - you can almost say it's inevitable. Many a beginner's video contains five minutes worth of nothing. The beginner forgets to press the start/stop button at the end, the recording therefore runs on happily, the camcorder films whatever is in front of it, even the dark interior of the camcorder bag.

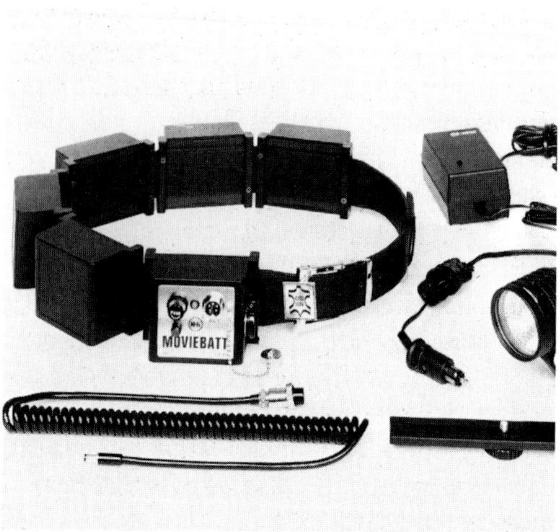

Power supply is the central problem for exterior shots with the camcorder. A quality battery pack belt is a most useful accessory when on the move.

Several minutes of this isn't just annoying - it unnecessarily wastes power from the battery pack. The one and only remedy is discipline. Get it into your mind: first stop the recording - the viewfinder will indicate Pause - then set down the camcorder from the eye.

A second unnecessary waste of power is also very common with beginners: you leave the camcorder in Pause mode and put it away somewhere. The camcorder will, of course, continue to use power: the viewfinder monitor is working, the head drum is rotating, the autofocus reacts to every movement in front of the front element and continually moves the focusing elements and/or the image converter.

Manufacturers have built a device into the camcorder which puts an end to this unnecessary waste after a few minutes. It simply switches off the camcorder, if only to spare the magnetic tape. Up to then you are wasting power.

So: switch off the camcorder as often as possible (Power button). Don't worry about missing anything wonderful: camcorders nowadays are ready too shoot very quickly after switching on - so you won't lose any snapshots.

The second serious way of wasting power is often simply by pleasing the children, partner or friend: "Oh, Daddy please, let me have a look at what you've filmed!" So Daddy switches to Recorder mode, rewinds the tape some way, presses the Play button (for playback), the children press an eye to the viewfinder eyepiece to watch the recording. Because only one person can look through the eyepiece at any one time, the whole process may be repeated several times, and it costs power! Not so serious, but still noticeable in terms of power consumption is frequent zooming - that is, changing the focal length with the zoom motor. (This sort of pseudo zooming is very popular with beginners. So don't do it: zooming in the picture is a pain!!) Why so much talk about power? Because the empty battery pack is the main cause of bitter disappointment in video filming.

"Switch off the camcorder as often as possible in order to save power"

You're completely wrong if you think that the central problem in video filming is the creation of ingenious picture compositions, or creative self-realization through a unique individual visual language not seen previously, or rhythmical editing full of tempo.

The biggest problem is power. Nothing works without power, and the best scenes and subjects always crop up when you've run out of juice. Then the camcorder switches off automatically. Remember; the smaller and lighter the camcorder, the smaller and lighter the battery pack, and the lower its capacity for storing power, and the shorter the recording length per battery pack charge.

The capacities of camcorder battery packs range from 1000 mAh (milliamperes per hour) to 2400 mAh. Manufacturers give a certain recording length per battery pack charge in the operating manual, but this is often arrived at in unrealistic conditions. Assume around a third of this time, and you will be about right. On mini-packs you can expect (as a rule of thumb) a recording time of approximately 30 minutes, on the very large ones (2400 mAh) perhaps one and a half to two hours. As you don't - I am assuming - waste power as described above, the real recording length per pack charge depends on the state of the pack, and how you treat it.

● Very new battery packs, or packs which have been stored unused for several months, only reach part of their original capacity; a battery pack only reaches its full potential after it has been completely discharged and recharged three to four times.

"The smaller the camcorder and the battery pack, the shorter the recording length per pack charge"

● A battery pack which has only been partially discharged and then recharged several times 're-members' this (memory effect); it then only delivers a proportion of its power.

● Every battery pack loses power naturally (self-discharge), but a particularly high amount if you leave it on the camcorder.

● Battery packs discharge themselves particularly rapidly in highly humid conditions (at or on the sea, in the tropics).

● The battery pack provides 20 to 40 per cent less power at very low temperatures (for example in winter sports).

What do we deduce from this?

1. The battery pack provided isn't even enough for an afternoon in the zoo, particularly if it (the battery pack) is almost new. Don't bother to leave the house without a spare charged battery pack.

2. Unpackaged battery packs and a bunch of keys (or other electrically conducting materials) don't belong in a bag together: this could lead to short circuiting.

3. Don't throw a battery pack on a table or the floor, even in a hurry; it could cause internal damage to its cells.

4. Before recharging it, ensure that every battery pack is completely discharged (the camcorder switches off).

Modern high-quality mains/charging units ensure that the inserted battery pack is completely discharged before recharging by means of a special feature (discharge). These mains/charging units are also capable of maintenance charging. The battery pack remains in the connected mains/charging unit; this controls the charging voltage so that the loss through self-discharge is neutralized, but no overcharging takes place. The battery pack is always in top form.

5. At temperatures below zero keep the singly wrapped battery packs (small plastic sacks) in the inside pocket of a coat so that they stay warm.

6. Before departing on trips to areas with high humidity, pack each battery pack separately in a small sealable plastic bag, adding silica gel sachets which absorb humidity.

It is a well-known fact that humidity causes condensation on cold surfaces. The camcorder has a highly polished rotating head drum

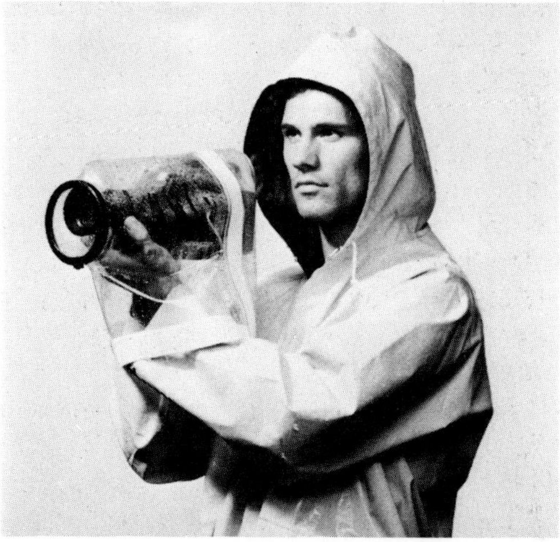

Heavy moisture spells danger for the camcorder. Protective covers from ewa marine allow video recording in bad weather conditions.

inside it. Now if, for example, you take your camcorder from the cold temperature outside into the cosy warmth of a ski hut, the humidity of the air causes condensation on the head drum because of the change in temperature.

The same happens if you're in the tropics and go from an air-conditioned room outside into the humid warm air. Tiny drops of water form on the head drum. Then what happens? If you switch the camcorder on, the indicator will show the letters DEW (for dew, humidity), and the camcorder switches itself off again.

And that's just as well: the humidity would cause the tape to stick to the head drum and, because this rotates at a very high speed, the tape would rip. The camcorder switches off until the humidity has evaporated completely. If you press the Eject button and take out the cassette the interior of the camcorder warms up quicker.

Earlier we touched on the subject of travelling. We do, of course, need to think about how to pack the camcorder plus accessories. To travel with a camcorder without protection would be sheer madness. Not just sand on the beach or a rainstorm, but the real possibility of transit damage. Hard-shell cases are available for camcorders and are the single best investment made by people on the move.

Some manufacturers deliver the camcorder in a carry case. These cases are not ideally suited for transport other than casual journeys in a car. Yes, try to check-in your camcorder as hand baggage for flights - but if it has to go into the hold of the plane you do need a proper hard-shell case, as a bag or flimsy carry case will not offer the required protection.

1. Taking the camcorder out of the case does not take long but it can be a nuisance; you've got to set the case down and might need both hands to take out the camcorder if it sits tightly in the made-to-measure foam shapes or dividers.

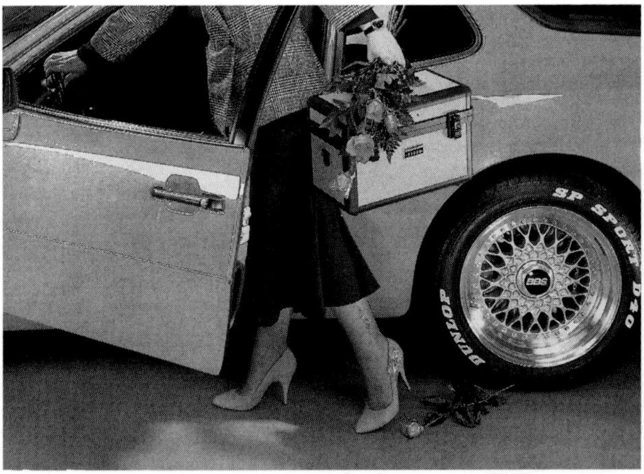

They are elegant as well as robust. Many types are available but the hard-shell Tundra/ Kinetics are best.

So you might well need a camcorder bag for video filming. If you're a sportsperson, enjoy cycling or cross-country skiing, you would be well-advised to get a camcorder bag which is fitted with a shoulder strap but can also be carried on the back as a rucksack.

Choose the bag carefully. It needs to be water-repellent, keep its shape and be rip-proof. As you will probably accumulate a certain amount of extra accessories, the bag needs to be of reasonable size, but the camcorder shouldn't flop about in it. So you need to take into account the design of interior compartments; it's best to take your camcorder with you when you buy. But above all, you should be able to take the camcorder out of the bag with one hand, without any messing about, quickly and easily. The best happens when you least expect it, and then you need to be ready to shoot fast.

Note: there are bags for smaller camcorders which are designed like a large pistol holster; they are carried on the belt and you can 'pull' quickly. Right, now you've come to grips with the technical trimmings, you know your camcorder inside out, and you're ready for video filming. Now you just need to be creative.

Learning to See with the Camcorder

Many very clever people have written at length in innumerable video film books on rules for creating videos. I don't believe in rules. In film, which is where video comes from after all, everything is possible. What I would suggest is:

- Don't make a single shot too short. First, the camcorder needs one to three-and-a-half seconds after you have started it until it can record. Second, it cuts off one to three seconds from the previous shot in order to join the next shot without faults (assemble edit).
- Don't hold the camcorder in front of the eye like a movie film camera. Tilt the viewfinder eyepiece upwards, look into it from above and give the camcorder additional support with the left hand. This has the following advantages: the camcorder (and therefore the image) shake far less, and you get away from the truly boring adult eye-level shot. This type of shot is terrible for children and small animals - get down to their level!

- Don't go mad on zooming and panning, particularly right at the beginning of a shot. First, this will give the viewers no chance of orientation ("Where on earth are we?"); and second you have no opportunities for editing. Therefore:
- start and finish with a still subject
- don't just take close-up shots of your wife
- if you do, she shouldn't keep bumping into the image edge or even run out of the frame. Select a more total shot (experts speak of $^{2}/3$-shots, that is, the person only fills $^{2}/3$ of the image area). This applies even more so to everything that moves quickly (animals, children).

There is more to say, but as you get to enjoy video filming you will get to know that as you go along. Just keep this in mind: however sophisticated (and expensive) your camcorder, it's you who makes the video, not the equipment. What does it depend on? On your learning to see - to see and create with a camcorder.

Converters: Changing the Focal Length

Focal length and angle of view are two physical terms which say something about the seeing ability of a lens. The essential characteristic of a lens is the focal length, for it decides the scale of reproduction and the image section. Many people find it confusing that a focal length of 48mm is supposed to be a big telephoto lens on a video camera. It is a standard lens on a normal 35mm camera. On medium format semi-professional cameras it would even be a super wide-angle lens. This can only be interpreted in relation to the recording angle and in comparison with the angle of view of the human eye. No matter whether it is a film, a tube or a chip, light falls onto reception surfaces of different sizes. The diagonal of this reception surface decides what is a standard, telephoto or wide-angle focal length. In all these cases the diagonal of the reception surface as the focal length provides an image which corresponds to the normal human angle of vision.

A 35mm camera lens can have a focal length of 50mm, and a camcorder lens one of 9mm with a 1/2" CCD chip. Both record an angle of view of 46° and therefore obtain identical image sections. For this reason you can always multiply the focal length of a camcorder by the factor 5.5 with a 1/2" CCD in order to get an idea how big such a lens would be in the area of 35mm photography. A video focal length of 70mm and a 1/2" CCD therefore corresponds to one of 385mm in 35mm photography.

But if you know that 9mm is the standard focal length, everything above 9mm is already a telephoto lens, and everything that is shorter than 9mm falls into the wide-angle range. All focal lengths above 9mm therefore have a narrower angle of view than the human angle of vision and consequently enlarge the subject.

All focal lengths below 9mm (on the camcorder) record a wider angle of view and record everything smaller, but get more of the subject into the frame overall.

As everything also happens proportionally, you can establish the enlargement factor in the telephoto range, as on a pair of binoculars, or the reduction factor in the wide-angle range. To do this, you simply have to divide the focal length by 9. A telephoto focal length of 72mm therefore enlarges the subject exactly eight times. It brings an object eight times closer (72 : 9 = 8), as close as with a pair of 8x binoculars.

However, because of the small size of the CCD chip it has so far not been possible to build lenses at acceptable prices and in adequate quality which can record a large wide-angle range. It is always a problem when you want to fill the frame with several people in an interior scene.

The two frames at the top show the different image section in the maximum telephoto setting of the integral camcorder lens (left).

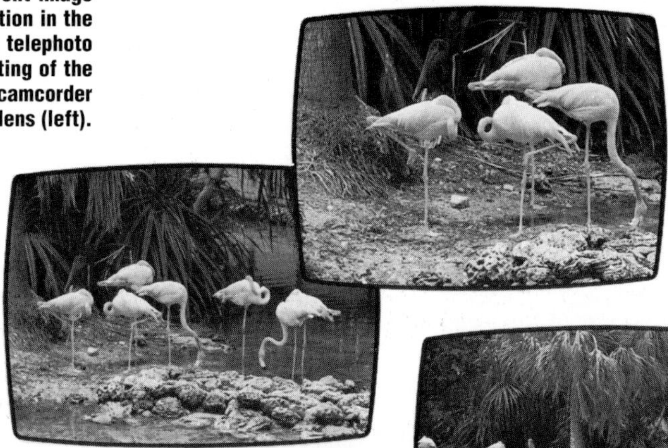

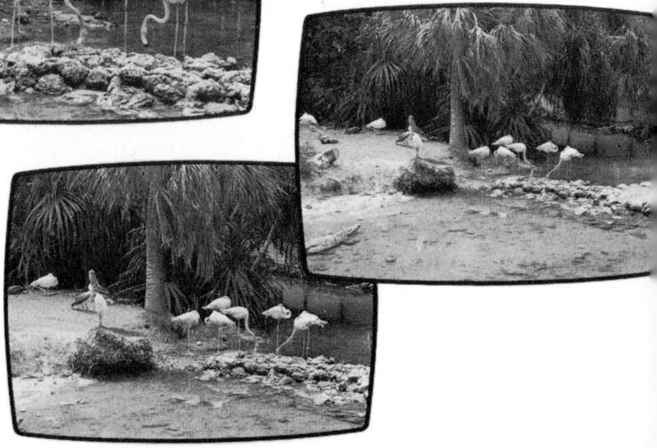

This is what the image section looks like in a normal wide-angle setting of the camcorder lens.

In the short term this can only be solved by a lens attachment. The wide-angle 0.5, which shortens the focal length of the camcorder by a factor of 0.5 and therefore doubles the angle of view, is ideal. It turns the 9mm standard focal length into a 4.5mm super wide-angle lens. Theoretically it also turns a 20mm telephoto into a 10mm telephoto lens. But why use this converter in the telephoto range when it is already available on the original lens? Also, every converter reduces the maximum performance of the lens. But in the wide-angle range there is no other way. Converters are screwed into the filter ring at the front of the lens, and can also be used with automatic focusing and exposure. For shots back in the telephoto range the converters should always be removed.

If for any reason the existing focal length of the camcorder lens isn't enough, you can also attach lens converters in the telephoto range. Some telephoto lens converters are available from the camcorder manufacturer. Accessory specialists offer lens attachments which increase focal lengths between 1.5 and 12 times. Such a 12x lens in conjunction with a 70mm telephoto setting is quite capable of recording a single crater on the moon to fill the frame. But this is hardly likely to succeed because the danger of camera shake increases by the same factor. Also, atmospheric conditions will rarely allow such strong enlargements to be recorded cleanly.

An 4x increase in the camcorder focal length is ideal for a safari in Africa, or for animal shots in a zoo. The sun at sunset is usually too large for this. You'll probably get it big enough for the edges to appear to melt into the atmosphere with a 1.5 or 2x converter. But all of that will work only if the shutter speed is reduced and a sturdy tripod is used. At focal lengths above 90mm hand-held shots in acceptable quality are guaranteed impossible. But even a sturdy monopod can, in conjunction with a converter, get a grown lion to fill the frame.

"At focal lengths above 90mm hand-held shots in acceptable quality are guaranteed to be impossible"

You should have the camcorder with you when you buy a converter in order to be able to screw on and test the attachment. When zooming through the whole range of the telephoto lens you should pay particular attention to the corners of the image, so that there is no undesirable darkening or vignetting (shading-off).

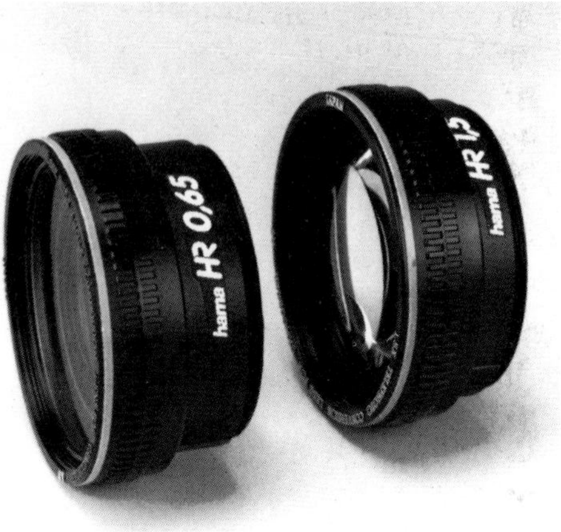

Extreme converters (from about 4x) should, in addition, be fitted with an extra lens support because the whole lens is supported only by the relatively small filter ring of the original lens. This will often not be enough. A light knock, a bump into the edge of the table or against the wall can be enough to break the lens attachment from the filter ring.

Telephoto and wide-angle attachments HR 0.65 and HR 1.5 from quality suppliers.

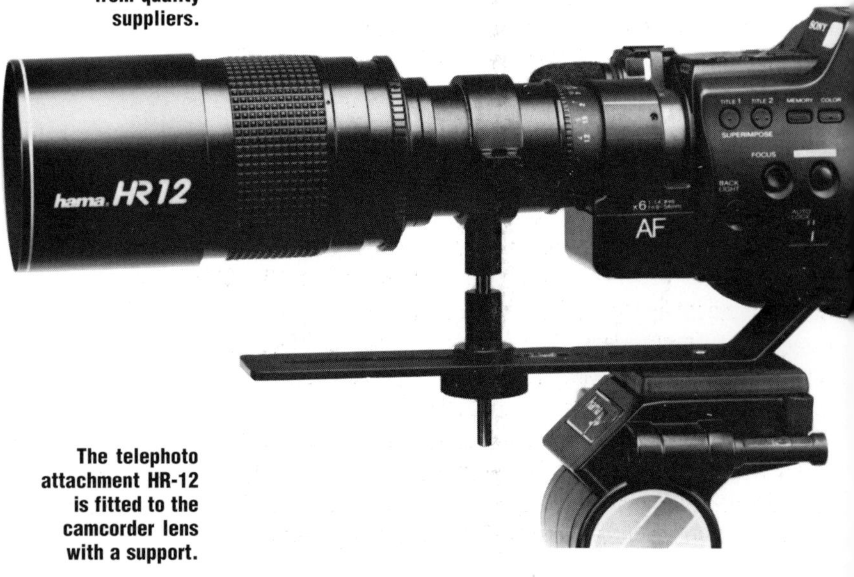

The telephoto attachment HR-12 is fitted to the camcorder lens with a support.

Close-up Attachments

Even if the camcorder has its own macro setting on the lens, a close-up lens , or better still an achromatic attachment, can be a highly effective accessory. The main problem in macro settings is the often extreme proximity to the subject, which is sometimes less than a millimetre away from the front element. The range beginning somewhere between 1.5 and 1 metres and ending at about 30cm from the lens is captured satisfactorily only by very few lenses. But there is a multitude of video subjects in this range in particular, and it can be an exciting experience to react to the small beauties of nature and to turn them into video scenes full of atmosphere.

The closer the video camera is to the subject, the more careful you need to be with focusing - because the depth of field reduces as the reproduction ratio increases. It is therefore sensible in the close-up range to keep the subject plane as parallel to the film plane as possible. So go ahead and point the camera straight down rather than capturing the scene with the camera at an angle. Look into the flower from directly above so that the graphic circular shape really is visible as a circle in the viewfinder. The sharpness is then also distributed evenly across the whole shot.

The attachment element is comparable with a spectacle lens which in this instance enables a usually long-sighted lens to see sharply in the close-up range. An achromat attachment, which is a small optical system in itself and therefore corrected, is qualitatively far superior. The close-up lens or achromat attachment are positive lenses which achieve their effect by reducing the focal length of the camera lens. The focal length becomes shorter, and the distance to the film is therefore optically increased. The lens now sees in the close-up range, but no longer as far as infinity.

The different strengths in dioptres quoted for close-up attachments stand for different distance ranges, with 1 being weaker than 2, and 2 weaker than 3; but 2 and 1 together make 3 and have the same effect as a close-up element of 3 dioptres. Just two elements

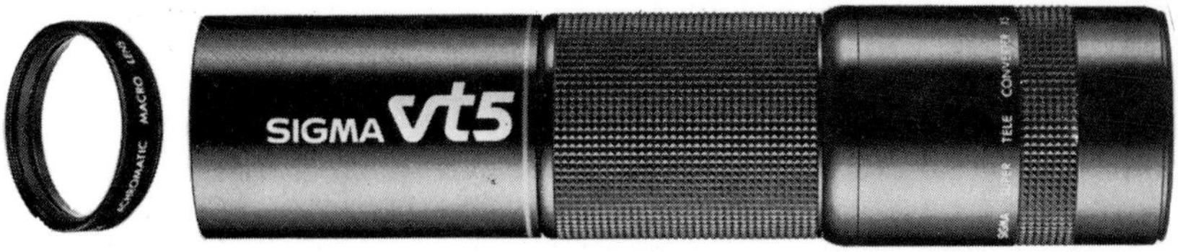

Telephoto converter and macro achromatic attachment for large reproductions of small subjects from a distance.

therefore allow subject distances of between about 150 and 25cm. The element with the strength of 1 suffices at infinity setting from 1m to 50cm (with the lens set to 1m), strength 2 from 50cm to about 33cm, and both together from 33cm to about 25cm. At this distance a postcard fills the frame. So in order to make optimum use of the close-up attachment you only have to remember the most distant and the closest point. The exact image section can easily be judged on the monitor, and be adapted to the ideas of the videographer by changing the focal length.

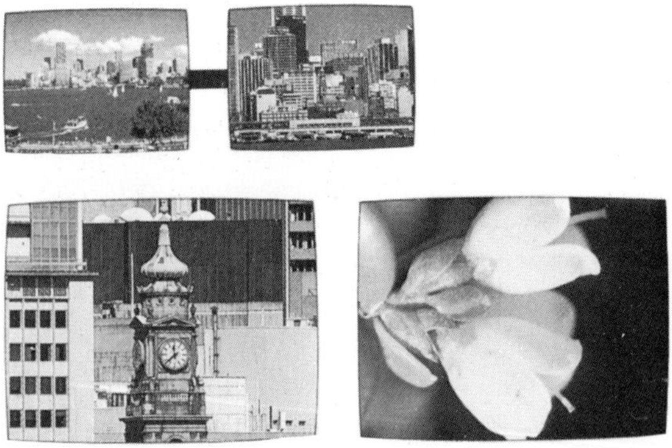

High-quality attachments can extend the wide-angle, telephoto and macro range.

Travelling with the Camcorder

Before you set off on a journey you will by now have read through this book carefully. You will know about the technical possibilities of your camcorder and have an understanding of lighting, sound; zooming, dollying and panning. Only a little more is required to ensure that your holiday film will be a perfect success and you come back happy.

Insurance

Video equipment is in demand by thieves. Insurance for the equipment is more than sensible. But even the best insurance policy doesn't cover all eventualities. If you don't want to miss out in case of a claim you should stick precisely to the guidelines, which are usually in small print. Travel insurance companies are more than careful in their claims policy. The reason: amateur fraudsters feel unobserved and safe in foreign countries and like to construe a case in their favour.

In many cases insurers refuse a claim by reasoning that the insured was grossly negligent. For example, you hang the bag with your equipment over the arm of your chair in an Italian restaurant in order to concentrate your efforts on fighting with the spaghetti. If a thief strikes in this situation you will usually end up losing out. According to current court verdicts you have behaved in a grossly negligent way. The same applies if a clever thief snatches the camcorder from Granny's lap while you're stopped at a red light. Valuables are hardly ever insured in the car. If the worst comes to the worst your only hope is the insurer's discretion, which can sometimes pay you a lump sum compensation for all the luggage disappeared from the car. Reporting the incident to the police is absolutely necessary as proof.

The insurance company will want a copy of the report made to the local police or at least details such as date and time as well as the name of the officer you spoke to and the address of the station. Your chances of appearing believable to the insurer are also increased by statements from official persons. You should try and get a lawyer to check the notification of a claim.

Well-equipped

When travelling, you should be well prepared for all eventualities. This includes:

● Two or more spare battery packs so that you don't run out of energy in the middle of the best scene on the beach, in the city, in field or forest;

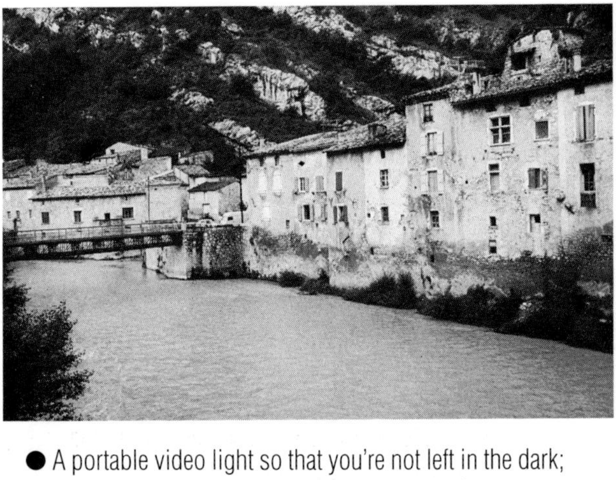

The best places for video films: your own "back-yard". But the world comes to your home when you travel with your camcorder.

● A portable video light so that you're not left in the dark;

● A dust brush and cleaning materials for the lens;

● Several sachets of silica gel which absorbs the humidity in tropical countries;

● A tripod or a good monopod;

● Enough spare tapes for the whole trip;

● A tape recorder for additional sounds to create an authentic atmosphere;

● Possibly an adaptor to cope with other TV standards (see below).

Other Countries, other Standards

In some countries the TV standard, like the voltage, varies. The TV standard in North America is very different to that in Europe.

If you plan to use your equipment in any country other than where the product was purchased, please check with a competent retailer who can advise you the best course of action to ensure no damage occurs by connection to unsuitable electricity sources.

Additional Tips

● You have to complete an import declaration on entering some countries. You should have your sales receipt for this - and enough money to leave a deposit, if required.

● As a precaution you should always check all important camcorder functions before departure.

● A camcorder is sensitive to dust, sand and humidity. It is best kept in a bag or hard-shell case. You should never leave it unprotected in the car or on the beach. A towel for protection is better than nothing.

● Different filters don't only help you achieve different special effects; a filter fully protects your lens against scratches and dust in 'down time'.

● Before connecting your equipment to the mains abroad, check whether the voltage is correct.

● If possible, try to carry your video equipment as hand luggage on plane journeys. If not, use a hard-shell case.

Maintenance and Care

Just like your car, your camcorder needs regular care and maintenance if it is to give you lasting enjoyment. The lens as well as the camera body and video cassettes need to be stored correctly and looked after. Your video equipment does not like humidity, dust, sand and strong sunlight. Direct light, from the sun as well as from lamps, damages camera and lens. Tapes, too, are very sensitive to heat. They can also be damaged by the proximity of magnetic fields. The camcorder does not cope well with shocks and bumps. Video equipment is best kept in a suitable bag or a sturdy hard-shell case for travelling.

Your video equipment is best carried in a suitable video bag and kept safe on travels in a hard-shell case. Not cheap, but a great investment.

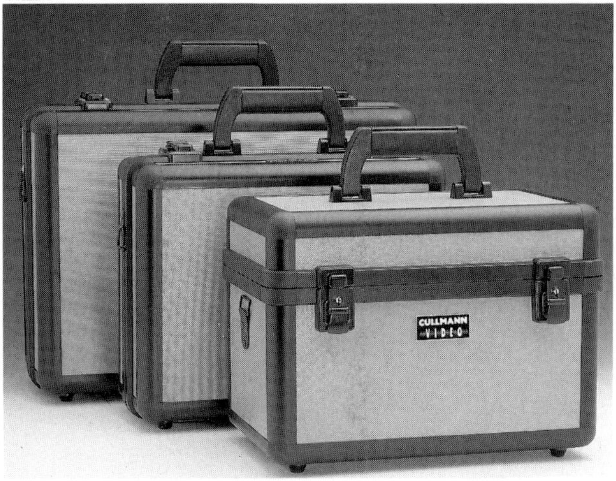

Heat and Humidity

If you go from a wintery ski piste into the warm hotel, tiny drops of water form on the surface of the camcorder. The cassette then needs to be taken out, the cassette compartment needs to stay open.

You must never use the camcorder before the condensation has evaporated. Depending on the surrounding humidity, this can take more than an hour. It is quicker if you put your camcorder in a plastic bag before such a temperature change. In this case you only need to wait until the machine has adjusted to room temperature before you can take it out. In rain, fog, humid climatic zones or on boat trips you can protect your camcorder against wetness and humidity with a transparent ewa-marine cover.

Well Looked After

Video cassettes should never be kept in the camcorder. They are best stored upright in a video cassette box. You should take the battery pack out before putting away the camcorder equipment for a long period of time. Inactivity over several months is not at all good for the equipment. So you should occasionally use the camcorder just to keep all the parts moving.

Dust and dirt also need to be removed from the camera and lens on a regular basis. The lens is best cleaned with a wet-wipe, an optical brush or a soft fluff-free cleansing cloth. You can also use the optical wipe to clean the viewfinder window of the camera.

You should periodically get your camcorder equipment cleaned and checked by experts. The video heads and head drum in particular need this kind of service. If they are dirty the image quality is reduced.

You should never try to carry out repairs yourself if malfunctions appear that can't be resolved by referring to the operating manual. If you use this DIY method you will usually do more harm than good. The expert will work out cheaper.

Extra Tips:

- Always use the specified battery packs!
- Don't connect the camcorder to incorrect voltages or connections!
- Whatever happens, always stick to the operating manual of the machine!

Glossary of Specialist Terms

(for a more detailed list of terms see *A-Z Camcorders and Video* by Michael Huber, Hove Foto Books. ISBN 0-906447-69-0)

A

Accumulator

Stores electrical current with the help of chemical processes. Batteries, on the other hand, produce current through chemical processes.

Acoustic feedback

An unpleasant whistling sound occurs when the switched-on camcorder is connected to the running TV set. The reason: a feedback circuit which continually amplifies itself is formed between the TV loudspeaker(s) and the camcorder microphone (and the relevant amplifiers). Best remedy: switching off the TV sound.

AGC

Short for automatic gain control. Weak signals are amplified up to a pre-selected value. On video shots with insufficient light, however, the interference signal is also amplified.

Assemble Edit

The joining of scenes recorded one after the other without image faults at the editing points.

Audio Dubbing

Specialist term for post sound recording.

Autofocus

A system in the camcorder which automatically sets the sharpness. However, on many models the autofocus does not work in the macro range, when there is too little light, and with infrared systems through glass, for example.

AV socket/jack

Socket/jack to connect video (image) and audio (sound) sources (video recorder, camcorder). There are different types of AV sockets/jacks: DIN-AV, EURO-AV (also called SCART), Phono/RCA sockets/jacks; S-VHS, S-VHS-C and Video Hi-8 equipment uses the combination of an S-socket/jack (Y/C) for the video signal and RCA/phono socket/jack (for the audio signal).

Axis jump

Regarded as a fault in picture composition. If, for example, two people stand facing each other and close-up shots of their faces are edited together, one person faces from left to right; when the camera jumps across the imaginary line (axis) between the two people, the second person also faces from right to left so, optically speaking, the two aren't talking to each other.

B

Backlight compensation

This is carried out automatically or by pressing the relevant button (usually labelled back light); this will open the iris diaphragm by approximately one stop. The purpose: subjects in backlight or in front of light backgrounds don't turn into black silhouettes but are shown with contrasts.

C

CCD

Short for Charge Coupled Device, the most frequently used semi-conductive image sensor; it converts light entering through the lens into electronic signals. The number of image points per unit area is decisive for the resolution capacity of the semi-conductive image sensor.

Colour temperature

Measured in kelvins. The distribution of colour in light. Daylight at noon has a larger proportion of blue, evening sunshine a larger red proportion. Artificial light sources have specific colour temperatures, too. Colour temperatures are defined according to the light emitted by a heated block of metal (the hotter, the more blue) - hence the name colour temperature.

Compatibility

Fitting together, in the mechanical or electronic sense or in software terms. Problems often arise because of different plugs and sockets/ jacks. If the machines work in the same TV standard, there are no problems in connecting camcorders, video recorders and TV sets via the aerial socket/jack. In S-VHS, S-VHS-C and Hi-8, however, optimum image quality is only reached with the S-socket/jack (also called Y/C socket/jack). A VHS cassette doesn't fit into a VHS-C camcorder, but a VHS-C cassette in an adaptor cassette fits and functions in a VHS recorder.

Video 8 cassettes can only be played back in Video 8 camcorders/ video recorders; because of their dimensions they don't fit into any other system, and the recording system is different. See the relevant articles on compatibility of Super-VHS on the one hand, and Video Hi-8 on the other.

The range of multi-standard colour TV sets which can receive all customary TV standards is continually increasing.

Video cassettes recorded in NTSC can't be played back on a PAL video recorder. There are, however, multi-standard home video recorders with standard conversion. If you frequently want to watch NTSC cassettes you should get a NTSC home recorder and connect it to a multi-standard colour TV set.

CTL track

Short for Capstan Tracking Logic. A longitudinal track along the tape edge onto which synch pulses are recorded to control the video heads during play-back. Time codes can also be recorded onto the CTL track; like frame numbers, these can mark single frames on the film for precise editing. When travelling abroad, if you buy a pre-recorded video you must check if it is suitable for use on your own country's system.

D

dB

Decibel, a logarithmic unit indicating the ratio between two power levels or two sound levels. 6dB means a doubling, 20dB a ten-fold, 40dB a 100-fold and 60dB a 1000-fold increase. A signal/noise ratio of 43dB often found on camcorders corresponds to a ratio of usable and interference signal of 101.41:1.

Diagonal track recording

All home video recorders and camcorders, and many professional image recording machines record the video signal (and often the audio signal, too, in which case it is hi-fi quality) diagonally to the direction the tape runs. This is done by means of two or more video heads on a rotating disc or drum, around which the magnetic tape is wound at 180° or more.

Dioptres setting

A ring on the viewfinder eyepiece allowing spectacle-wearers to adjust the image in the viewfinder monitor to their individual visual acuity.

Dropout

Flashes appear in the image, or the sound crackles during play-back of videos; this is caused by the usable signal momentarily cutting out. The reason: faults in the magnetic layer, or contaminations sticking to the magnetic layer.

DEW

Accumulation of moisture on the camcorder mechanics, caused by extremely high humidity or condensation (fast transition between cold and warm). The camcorder indicates DEW and switches off until the moisture has dried, otherwise the magnetic tape would stick to the rotating head drum and tear.

E

Edit socket/jack

Used for the connection of a control lead between camcorder and video recorder, or between two video recorders. When play-back is started on one machine, the record function of the other one is started simultaneously.

Editing

The name used for the electronic cutting of video recordings. A play-back device (Player) and a recording device (Recorder) are always required for editing.

Edit search

A feature on the camcorder allowing you to search for a particular frame in the previous shot to join a new shot, without the need to even leave record mode.

Euro-AV connection (also called SCART)

21-pole connection between TV sets and video machines to carry image and sound. Some manufacturers also include Euro-AV sockets/jacks in S-VHS, S-VHS-C and Video Hi-8 camcorders.
Warning: some SCART leads are only connected for one-way usage, which is fine from camcorder to video/TV, but a two-way lead would be required for most other uses.

Exposure control

Often indicated by the abbreviation EXP or AE (Automatic Exposure); it regulates the amount of light reaching the image sensor by opening or closing the iris diaphragm. The most common system is a fully automatic exposure control program which can be switched off. Improvements in automatic exposure control are achieved by means of multiple field metering and fuzzy logic.

F

Fade

A command for blending video (image) and often also audio (sound) in and out.

Flying erase head

Erase head mounted on the rotating head drum with the video heads. Whereas a rigid erase head erases across the whole tape and therefore removes signals across several diagonal tracks, the flying erase head only erases the required diagonal tracks. There are no image faults at the editing points. Insert editing is only possible with a flying erase head.

Focal length

A bundle of light rays reaching a lens in parallel to its optical axis converge in the focal point after passing through the lens. The focal length is the distance between the centre of the lens and the focal point.

Because of the different reproduction ratios you need to multiply the selected focal length of a camcorder with a $^1/2$" CCD chip by 5 (rule of thumb) when comparing the focal lengths of camcorder and photographic camera. This will give the corresponding focal length of a 35mm photographic camera.

Fuzzy logic

A functional principle from computer technology. Whereas logic connections were previously only capable of the states 'yes' or 'no', fuzzy logic allows the control of electronic connections with less definite (fuzzy) commands. A fuzzy logic circuit can work with commands such as 'a little' or 'perhaps'. It is used on camcorders, together with multiple field metering, in automatic programs for sharpness, exposure control and the white balance, so that they function in a way that is closer to the way the human eye sees (Human Eye Logic).

H

Hi-8

A video system in high-quality camcorders. A substantial increase in the frequency of the brightness (luminance) signal and the separate processing of the brightness and colour signals, plus special magnetic tape and amorphous video heads achieve the following:

● The resolution rises to more than 400 lines. Image faults through dubbing (cross over) are reduced. The interference signal (noise) does not increase, but is more likely to decrease, despite the higher resolution.

For optimum play-back of Hi-8 recordings the Hi-8 camcorder needs to be connected to a colour TV set with S-socket/jack (also called Y/C socket/jack).

HQ

Short for High Quality; connection with VHS and VHS-C machines, firstly to reduce the interference signal (noise) and secondly, for better marginal sharpness in the image, particularly on dark/bright transitions.

I

Insert edit

The joining of a new scene into a scene already recorded, without image faults at the editing points.

Intermediate edit

An intermediate edit shows shots designed for extra explanation of the action, for example places the participants are talking about at the time.

J

Jitter

Mechanical vibration of the magnetic tape when running around the head drum in the video recorder/camcorder; produces unsharp vertical edges in the image and roughness of the sound in longitudinal track recordings.

L

LCD

Short for Liquid Crystal Display, used on the camcorder as an additional indicator panel. Camcorders with colour LCD displays have become available very recently.

Light intensity

It is measured in Lux. The camcorder manufacturer indicates the minimum light intensity required for recording (for example 7 Lux). Many manufacturers also indicate a standard light intensity (for example 800 Lux) at which the camcorder produces images which are true to the original colours and to a large extent noise-free.

Line jump method

This is designed to keep down the flickering of the image on the TV screen during play-back. It works by separating the TV image into two semi-images, with the odd line numbers written before the even ones. This doubles the image change frequency.

Long Play (LP)

Operating mode which halves the tape speed, and therefore doubles the recording length of the inserted cassette, found on many camcorders and home video recorders. The machine automatically recognizes the operating mode used on recorded cassettes; if the machine allows Long Play operation, it automatically switches to the relevant mode. If it doesn't, it can't play back cassettes recorded in Long Play mode. The image quality is reduced in LP (more noise); but the reduction in quality is low on S-VHS, S-VHS-C and Hi8 camcorders. Special types of play-back, such as still image, single frame advance, slow motion and frame search produce a worse image in LP mode, or are not possible at all. The sound quality is only reduced in Long Play operation if the sound was recorded (exclusively) on the longitudinal track.

M

Macro setting

Allows very small subjects to be filmed to fill the frame. The macro range starts at varying distances from the front lens. The autofocus system does not work in the macro range on all camcorder models. In telephoto macro setting you are working with a telephoto focal length to take close-up shots of small subjects.

ME tape

Short for Metal Evaporated: tape material for the Video Hi-8 system, in which pure metal particles are sublimed onto the carrier foil in high vacuum conditions.

P

Post sound recording (audio dubbing)

Adding music, sounds or commentary to video recordings after filming. This is possible in the camcorder itself if the sound was (also) recorded on the longitudinal track (as in VHS, VHS-C, S-VHS and S-VHS-C), or on PCM tracks (high-quality Video 8 and Video Hi-8 camcorders), and if the camcorder has the Audio Dub facility. Otherwise post sound recording is possible only by copying to a second video recorder.

R

RF modulator

Used for connecting the camcorder to the aerial socket/jack of the TV set or home video recorder and usually comes with the camcorder. The audio/video signal of the camcorder is converted to look like a signal from the TV transmitter and raised to the UHF range (channels 30 to 40).

REC.REV

Short for Recording Review. In Record/Pause mode the last two to three seconds of the previous shot are played back.

Resolution capacity

The ability of depicting detail in the image. It is stated as the number of lines or as frequency in megahertz (MHz).

The important indication is the horizontal resolution. The following rule of thumb applies for converting lines to megahertz: number of lines divided by 80 is approximately equal to resolution in MHz; MHz x 80 is approximately equal to resolution in lines.

Record protect

Prevents accidental re-recording of video cassettes. On VHS and VHS-C cassettes it is a tab which can be broken off, on Video 8 cassettes it is a small switch.

S

Scan gap

The image on the TV monitor is produced by an electron beam which writes horizontally line by line by inducing phosphor particles located on the inside of the frontal screen of the picture tube to glow. Most of the energy is removed from the electron beam during the (horizontal or vertical) jump to the beginning of the next line to be written; it is scanned so that it cannot write during this jump (which would cause interference in the image). This is called the scan gap. It can be used for the transport of signals which are recognized and processed by a relevant decoder: video text on a TV station, for example, or VITC (Vertical Interval Time Code) on the camcorder.

Semi-images

(Also see *Scan gap*): in the CCIR/PAL TV standard 50 semi-images per second are written on alternating lines (lines 1, 3, 5 and so on, then lines 2, 4, 6 an so forth). The video/audio signals for a semi-image are contained on one video track; two tracks therefore produce a full image. With the NSTC standard the figure is 60 semi-images per second.

Shot

Continuous, uninterrupted film or video recording. Electronic high speed shutter allows the sharp reproduction of moving subjects and prevents unsharp movements during panning.

Smear effect

If a point-shaped light source shines into the lens, it causes a vertical coloured stripe in the image. The reason: the pixels (image elements, see *CCD*) on the image sensor reached by the ray of the light source are overloaded. On camcorders of the latest generation the smear effect is reduced to such a degree that it is negligible.

Sound recording

All camcorders record the original sound in synch with the image. There are different methods of analogue sound recording:
- with a rigid sound head on the longitudinal track of the tape edge
- with a moving sound head mounted on the rotating head drum, on the same diagonal tracks where the image signal is recorded.

Digital sound recording is only used on high-quality Video 8 camcorders and Video Hi-8 camcorders at present; this is also carried out by rotating heads on separate parts of the diagonal tracks.

In principle, all three methods are mono and stereo compatible. The sound quality is low in longitudinal track recording. For the sake of compatibility, VHS machines always use the longitudinal track method as well, even if diagonal track sound recording is available on the machine. The diagonal track method surpasses the hi-fi standard, reaching a frequency range from 20 to 20,000 Hz.

Video 8 camcorders use sound recording with a moving sound head on the diagonal track; stereo recording is customary on high-quality Video 8 camcorders. Longitudinal track recording is not available on Video 8.

If the sound is recorded only on the diagonal track, post sound recording in the camcorder itself is not possible because the video and audio signals are inextricably linked.

On top-quality Video 8 camcorders the sound is simultaneously recorded in analogue mode on diagonal tracks and digitally on separate tracks.

Digital recording almost reaches CD quality. Post sound recording is possible on the digital tracks.

Standard Play

An operating mode with the tape speed and video track width determined by the relevant standard.

Superimpose

A feature on high-quality camcorders which works as follows: you record a still image, for example a title graphic, before the actual recording. This is digitally stored in the camcorder and can then be imposed into the running shot at any time during video filming.

Super-VHS (S-VHS for short)

A system in the VHS and VHS-C format. Technical changes such as:

- broadened frequency range of the brightness (luminance) signal (from 1 MHz to 1.6 MHz)

- transposing the light density signal into a range between 5.4 MHz and 7 MHz (Standard VHS: 3.4 - 4.4 MHz)

- improved tape material (S-cassettes)

- a new type of video head (made from so-called amorphous material)

- a new way of signal processing (separate processing of brightness and colour signal)

resulted in the following improvements:

- the resolution increased to around 400 lines

- image faults due to cross interference were reduced.

For optimum play-back of S-VHS and S-VHS-C recordings the compatible camcorder needs to the connected to a colour TV set equipped with an S- (or Y/C) socket/jack.

S-VHS and S-VHS-C are compatible with standard VHS as follows:

- recorded VHS cassettes can be played back in S-VHS recorders (automatic switching)

- S-VHS machines can be switched to record in standard VHS (automatic switching)

- S-VHS cassettes can be recorded in standard VHS.

But cassettes recorded in S-VHS can't be played back on a standard VHS machine; this produces image faults which are so substantial that you can hardly recognize what you have recorded.

Synch pulses

These control the scanning electron beam in the TV set (see *Semi-image*) and are delivered by the TV transmitter. The home video recorder or camcorder records the synch pulses on a special synch - CTL - track.

T

Tape speed

Transport speed of the magnetic tape. In the PAL/CCIR norm it is a standard 2.339cm/s on VHS, S-VHS, VHS-C and S-VHS-C; on Video 8 and Video Hi-8 it is 2.0051cm/s. (Also see *Long Play*.)

Tape width

A) The width of the magnetic tape used in the video recorder/camcorder. This is 1/2" = 12.65mm on VHS, VHS-C, Super-VHS, Super-VHS-C, Beta and Video 2000; it is 8mm on Video 8 and Video Hi-8.

B) The area between the lowest and highest frequency broadcast, recorded and able to be scanned. It is given in hertz (Hz). 1 hertz (Hz) = 1 oscillation per second; 1 kilohertz (kHz) = 1000 oscillations per second; 1 megahertz (MHz) = 1 million oscillations per second. (Also see *S-VHS and Video Hi-8.)*

Time code

Signal for marking video images. Also see *VITC*.

Tracking speed

In diagonal track recording/play-back, the relative speed between the tape and the video/audio head mounted on the rotating drum.

V

VITC

Vertical Interval Time Code allows precise editing of video films. With VITC the information is written in the vertical scan gap of the video image (see *Scan gap, Semi-image* and *Time code*).

W

White balance

The white balance (WB for short) is necessary for natural colours in the image. It is controlled fully automatically on camcorders, but can also be carried out manually. (Also see *Colour temperature*.)

Z

Zoom

A lens with continuously variable focal length. 6x zoom lenses (shortest focal length x 6 = longest focal length) are typical; there are also 8x, 10x and 12x zoom lenses. Focal length adjustment is carried out by a motor when the relevant zoom button is pressed, or manually with the zoom lever.